Authentic Materials Myths

Applying Second Language
Research to Classroom Teaching

EVE ZYZIK

University of California, Santa Cruz

CHARLENE POLIO

Michigan State University

University of Michigan Press
Ann Arbor

The authors would like to thank Kelly Sippell for her continued help and enthusiasm from the time we approached her with the idea for this book until its final stages. Her advice, feedback, and ability to find outstanding reviewers have greatly shaped this book. Of course, we are extremely grateful to those reviewers who helped us develop the myths and provided supportive yet constructive feedback. In addition, we thank Senta Goertler, Jongbong Lee, Patricia Lunn, Jason Martel, and Ji-Hyun Park for their help at various stages during the preparation of this book.

♾ Printed on acid-free paper

ISBN-13: 978-0-472-03646-2 (paper)
ISBN-13: 978-0-472-12340-7 (ebook)

2020   2019   2018   2017   4   3   2   1

Contents

Introduction

Most language teachers would probably agree that using authentic materials is desirable. *Authenticity* is unequivocally a positive attribute: We value authenticity in cuisine, artwork, and merchandise. By the same token, authentic materials in language classrooms are prized as accurate and reliable representations of the target language. Nevertheless, there is considerable disagreement with respect to what kinds of authentic materials should be used, how they should be used, when they should be used, and how much of the curriculum should revolve around them. Even defining what constitutes something authentic is a matter of debate. In a book about using authentic materials, defining *authentic* must no doubt be the first task at hand, so this is where we begin.

Definition of Authentic Materials

Gilmore (2007), in his review of authentic materials, provided several definitions that were used over the years but eventually settled on one from Morrow (1977, cited in Gilmore, 2007), which defines authentic materials as "a stretch of real language, produced by a real speaker or writer for a real audience and designed to convey a real message of some sort" (p. 98). Noting that this definition includes a wide variety of language (including teacher-talk in the classroom), we opt for this modified definition:

> Authentic materials are those created for some real-world purpose other than language learning, and often, but not always, provided by native speakers for native speakers.

We use this definition to ensure that the language found in such materials is not modified for second language (L2) learners and has the primary intent of communicating information.

This definition, too, is not without problems for two reasons. First, words like *authentic, real,* and *native speaker* tend to be evaluative. The point of this book is not to argue that non-authentic materials (i.e., those created for language learning purposes) are without merit, but rather that authentic materials are essential and can be used much more broadly than most teachers might envision. Materials created by proficient non-native speakers are quite common in some contexts where English is a lingua franca (i.e., where it is used as a common language among speakers who have other first languages) and are therefore included in our definition of authentic materials. Second, even with this definition, gray areas exist, and it is important to discuss the possible benefits of such materials for language teaching. On a final note, we will use the terms *text* and *materials* interchangeably throughout the remainder of this book. However, *text* generally refers to any spoken or written language that is part of a set of materials. *Materials* is a slightly broader term that includes texts but also, for example, may simply be a set of pictures without any language.

Types of Authentic Texts

Authentic texts comprise both spoken and written language samples. For example, newspaper articles, short stories, advice columns, magazine ads, and graphic novels are commonly used authentic written texts. Spoken texts include, but are not limited to, television commercials, movies, radio broadcasts, lectures, songs, podcasts, and conversations or service encounters among native speakers. This last category would fall under what Wagner (2014) has called *unscripted texts*. He argued that unscripted oral texts contain additional features not found in scripted texts such as television shows. These types of texts would certainly fall under our definition of authentic, but they are much more difficult to collect.

The internet is a plentiful source of authentic texts that are not limited to one modality. We do not address multimodal texts (e.g., websites with audio and video) specifically, but most of the principles in this book apply to such texts. Even less text-laden materials—such as train schedules, menus, and nutrition labels—are unambiguously authentic. There remain some texts that may be useful but deserve additional discussion. These include teacher-made materials, children's books and graded readers, translations, and materials written for lingua franca contexts. We address each of these in turn.

Consider the following example of a teacher-made text. There is a unit in the textbook on food in the target culture, so the teacher interviews several native speakers about common foods found in their country. The interviews would be an excellent supplement, but would not fall under what we consider authentic texts because the speakers—in this case the people being interviewed—might naturally modify their speech when talking to non-native speakers, the students. In addition, there is no real-world activity associated with such an interview. If the teacher did not tell the interviewees what the recording was for, the language used might have been different, but there is still no real-world purpose that would guide the speakers. These types of materials are examples of useful texts, but ones that we do not consider in this book.

Children's books and graded readers are sometimes considered authentic. Many teachers use children's books because, intuitively, the language seems simpler. Nevertheless, children's books should be used with caution because they sometimes include slang, language play, and inaccessible cultural information. If teachers find appropriate children's books and note that their students enjoy such materials, the texts can be used as supplements. Graded readers for children, by definition, control the grammar and vocabulary used. One of the authors (Charlene) enjoyed using graded Chinese readers while studying Chinese in Taiwan because Chinese characters were added gradually, and because the books were replete with cultural information. Interested readers can also see Cho and Krashen (1994) in which adults became enthusiastic readers of a children's book series. The authors argue for the value of using such materials with adults. We will not, however, be considering the use of children's books or graded readers here.

Translated texts are an interesting matter. These materials are intended for native speakers for a certain purpose, such as the enjoyment of a movie, but the cultural references are often not related to the target culture. For example, should a Spanish instructor in the U.S. use the Spanish version of a popular U.S. television show such as *Friends*? Should a French teacher ask students to read *Harry Potter* in French? We think that such translations should definitely be considered authentic in that they serve as a vehicle for real language that native speakers would be engaged with. In addition, students often have the background knowledge to understand the materials. When Charlene was living in China, she could not understand Chinese television shows or movies very well. One day, a U.S. made-for-TV movie with an easy-to-follow plot was on, and she found she could understand much more. Similarly, she found that it was easy for her Chinese students to understand stories about China written in the English newspaper *The China Daily*. Thus, we recommend using these types of materials, but only with the caveat that they do not include information about the target culture.

Finally, we address the very complex issue of materials created for contexts in which the target language is the lingua franca—namely, a situation in which native speakers of two different languages use English to communicate because it is their common language. For example, speakers of two Asian languages such as Thai and Japanese often speak English in multinational companies. It is also likely that workplace materials such as emails are written in English. In a context such as Hong Kong or Singapore, the situation is more complex in that the creator of the materials might speak a local dialect of English but the listener is a second language learner. These dialect issues surface as well in Spanish materials produced in the U.S., such as a McDonald's menu, where the Spanish used may be different from the Spanish found in Spain or Mexico. We don't address these issues in this book, but we want to mention that they will be a factor in choosing which materials to use. Such materials are clearly authentic and have real-life purposes, but should also be considered carefully for each instructional context.

Authentic Texts in an Historical Context

Authentic texts have been used in language classrooms since the early days of the grammar-translation method, which was aimed at teaching students to read (and translate) literary texts. However, as language teaching methods evolved, the status of authentic materials also shifted. In other words, the perceived usefulness of authentic materials is closely linked to the dominant pedagogical approach of the time. For example, in the audiolingual method, authentic texts were dismissed in favor of a bottom-up approach beginning with sounds, words, phrases, and moving up to sentences, dialogues, and paragraphs. When Krashen's natural approach (Krashen & Terrell, 1983) achieved popularity, the focus was on comprehensible input or input that was just a bit above the students' level (i+1). Thus, using authentic texts with beginners was not advocated unless the teacher could find just the right materials. In other words, authentic texts were not excluded per se, but they could not be too difficult. The communicative approach, which advocated a focus on communicative competence, certainly took a favorable view toward authentic texts, particularly because these materials could help learners achieve sociolinguistic and discourse competence.

Most recently, and especially in foreign language contexts, there has been a general trend toward integrating language and content at all levels of instruction, as advocated by the Modern Language Association (MLA). The impact of the MLA report (2007) has been an increased use of literary texts in lower-level language courses with the goal of increasing students' cultural knowledge and analytical skills.

Authentic texts can also be discussed in relation to content-based and task-based teaching. In 1989, in a seminal book on content-based instruction, Brinton, Snow, and Wesche presented different models of content-based teaching that might use authentic texts to varying degrees, although the emphasis in Brinton et al. is clearly on authentic texts in every model. (This book was reissued in 2003.) They said specifically that language teaching materials can be used in conjunction with authentic texts but that "these materials must be selected carefully for their relevance to the course objectives" (p. 92). However, they defined content-based instruction more narrowly than others might; they used the term to refer to *sustained content* (e.g., a history class taught in Spanish) in contrast to textbook units or classes that address different topics throughout the course. Because of the varying definitions of content-based instruction, our focus in this book is on exploiting authentic texts in a variety of contexts, but we want to emphasize that using authentic texts is a way to integrate language and content.

Authentic texts can also play a central role in task-based instruction. In Willis' (2004) comprehensive review of task-based instruction, she noted that among the various definitions of tasks, the commonality is that they have an outcome or that there is a goal to achieve (see also Van den Branden, 2006, who came to the same conclusion). In addition, Skehan (1998) has suggested that tasks have some real-world relationship, meaning that the kind of discourse that arises during the task resembles naturally occurring discourse (Ellis, 2003, calls this *interactional authenticity*). Most importantly, tasks can incorporate authentic texts at various points in a lesson. Norris (2009) describes a task-input phase in which the target task is introduced "as it is realized in actual communication" (p. 583) without manipulation. For example, if the target task is buying a train ticket at a Madrid train station, a student could start by listening to authentic announcements, reading a train schedule, or better yet, listening to an authentic service encounter in the train station. (This last example, however, highlights the difficulty of getting access to native speakers completing real-world tasks.) Norris goes on to discuss pedagogic tasks using authentic texts. Pedagogic tasks are activities that are different from real-world tasks and can include something like a cloze activity or a jigsaw reading. We provide examples of pedagogic tasks as well as more traditional exercises throughout this book to show what teachers can do with authentic texts to make them comprehensible and usable to language learners.

Why Use Authentic Texts?

When teachers are asked about their rationale for using authentic texts, a common response is that students are motivated by them. Students have various reasons for studying a language (including satisfying a requirement), but the majority of students ultimately want to be able to communicate with native speakers, either locally or abroad. Accordingly, authentic texts may bring students closer to this goal by giving them a tangible sense of how the language is used in concrete situations. Although we certainly don't deny that authentic texts can motivate students, the relationship between authenticity and motivation is not as straightforward as we might assume. In fact, authentic texts that are too challenging for the students and not properly presented by the teacher will likely result in frustration rather than enhanced motivation. For example, Busse (2011) documented how university students in the U.K. became less motivated to learn German partially as a result of struggling with difficult German literature. These results are not entirely surprising: we cannot be motivated by texts that we don't understand. Indeed, it may be the sense of accomplishment that comes from understanding authentic texts that results in greater motivation. Viewed in this way, authentic texts are not inherently motivating; it is the process of understanding (and enjoying) authentic texts that helps language learners to feel more confident in their abilities, which results in increased motivation. As Gilmore (2007) explains, "The success of any particular set of authentic materials in motivating a specific group of learners will depend on how appropriate they are for the subjects in question, how they are exploited in class (the tasks) and how effectively the teacher is able to mediate between the materials and the students" (p. 107).

Another powerful reason for using authentic texts is that they provide richer input than textbooks or other instructional materials designed for language learners. Although the quality of textbooks can vary, research on English as a second language (ESL) and foreign language textbooks has consistently shown mismatches between textbooks and natural language use. First, textbooks often present a distorted view of grammar, overemphasizing certain structures at the expense of others (Goodall, 2010). In aiming to provide simple grammatical rules, textbooks may fall short of presenting fully accurate descriptions of language. Words and phrases, too, can be underrepresented. For example, Simpson-Vlach and Ellis (2010) compiled an academic phrase list from an oral and a written corpus. One of the phrases on their list from oral academic language was *blah, blah, blah*. We feel confident that this is not the type of phrase that would appear in a scripted lecture for an academic listening textbook.

An additional problem is the fact that textbooks generally present little information about pragmatically appropriate language use. Speech acts (e.g., giving advice, expressing agreement, making suggestions), as presented in textbooks, may differ quite dramatically from how they are realized in real-life conversations. One example of this is a study by Eisenchlas (2011), who compared advice-giving as presented in intermediate Spanish textbooks to online interactions. She found that textbooks seriously underrepresented the range of linguistic resources that Spanish-speakers use to give advice and gave no information regarding the pragmatic norms that underlie such interactions in the target culture. Consequently, researchers who study second language pragmatics have argued strongly for authentic texts as a way of providing learners with models of language that exemplify social, cultural, and discourse conventions.

Another reason to use authentic texts is that they provide a vehicle for integrating language and content and form and meaning. As mentioned, the MLA report (2007) advocated more integration of language and content, but at the lower levels, instructors may struggle with making content in authentic texts comprehensible to lower-proficiency students. At the higher levels, instructors may focus too much on content and too little on the language found in the texts (e.g., as found in Pica, 2002, and Polio & Zyzik, 2009). Thus, we emphasize throughout this book the importance of bringing more content to beginners and more language-focused instruction to advanced students through the use of authentic texts. Our recommendations stem from the understanding shared by many SLA researchers that learners need opportunities to focus on language forms (e.g., pronunciation, vocabulary, grammar), but not in isolation from meaningful language use. This is what Spada (1997) called *form-focused instruction*, defined as "pedagogical events which occur within meaning-based approaches to L2 instruction but in which a focus on language is provided in either spontaneous or predetermined ways" (p. 73). In this sense, authentic texts encourage a focus on meaning (e.g., understanding a message created for a real-world purpose), but teachers can intervene in various ways to provide the much-needed attention to language form.

A final argument that has been used to advocate for authentic texts is that they are associated with some real-world purpose. In task-based language teaching, as previously mentioned, it is vital to expose students to authentic texts that learners will encounter while doing real-world tasks. However, as will be discussed in Myth 7, what one does with an authentic text in a class may not resemble what one does with the text in real life. For example, students may be able to understand only a few words or sentences from a newspaper article, but a teacher might create an activity in which students have to match headlines and stories. Arguably, this is something no one would do in real life, but it is an excellent way of increasing students' familiarity with authentic texts and developing reading strategies such as skimming and scanning.

Practical Problems

There are a myriad of problems that come with using authentic materials as well, not the least of which is that it is time-consuming to find appropriate authentic texts and to then create good activities to accompany them. Of course, it's easy to say that teachers can share and reuse texts and activities, but one benefit of authentic texts is that they are often timely and so it's not clear how long they can be used. One solution is to fully exploit a text and use it with a variety of activities, sometimes even over the course of a semester. In addition, once you decide on some successful activities with your students (e.g., dictogloss, cloze, sentence ordering), you can quickly recreate these activities using new texts.

Choosing topics and texts is no easy task. Topics can be related to the students' interests (e.g., animé in a U.S. Japanese class), textbook topics (e.g., Mexican artists in a U.S. Spanish class), or students' needs (e.g., reading an academic journal article in an English for Academic Purposes class). There is no rule of thumb for choosing a text at the right level of difficulty because it depends on what one does with text. Throughout this book, we provide examples of activities that can be used with texts at a variety of levels in relation to students' proficiency. Thus, a related problem is deciding what to do with a text. For example, suppose you happen to have an attractive menu from the target culture that contains numerous dishes you have been discussing in class. Students will likely be interested in such realia, but what then is an appropriate activity or task? This is an issue we address throughout the book.

Finally, we must mention copyright issues when using authentic materials. First, copyright issues in general should not be seen as a barrier to using authentic texts in the classroom. Many of the ways you would use texts in your classroom will fall under fair use rules (http://www.copyright.gov/fls/fl102.html). Second, should you wish to publish materials in a course pack or textbook, permission to use authentic texts can usually be obtained, sometimes with no fee. If you need more information about copyright issues, you can begin with the U.S. government website (http://www.copyright.gov) or a university web site such as the one at Stanford University (http://fairuse.stanford.edu). Many U.S.-based universities have copyright librarians who can assist you in understanding the copyright laws and in applying for copyright permission. In addition, most websites have a terms of use or a terms-of-service link where you can obtain more information about using materials from a website.

Organization of the Book and Intended Audience

In preparing the proposal for this book, we began by generating a list of myths based on our collective experience in working with language teachers who try to integrate authentic materials and who have had varying degrees of success. Subsequently, based on feedback from the reviewers, we revised our list of myths. For example, we had originally intended to include a chapter on use of the L1, which some teachers believe should be strictly avoided when working with authentic materials. However, upon further reflection, we opted to eliminate this myth since it may not be very widespread. We also planned on writing a chapter to refute the idea that "only authentic texts should be used for language learning," but again, there may be few practitioners who hold this extreme view. Instead, we decided to include this topic in the Epilogue in order to emphasize that non-authentic materials also have a place in the curriculum, depending on the goals of the course and the needs of the students.

This book is organized in a similar way to the other Myths books in the University of Michigan Press series in that each chapter starts with an actual real scenario **(In the Real World)** and then is followed by a discussion of the research **(What the Research Says)**. Note that there is not a large amount of research using authentic materials, so we have often had to extrapolate from research using non-authentic materials when discussing possible instructional techniques. Each chapter also includes specific implications for the classroom **(What We Can Do)**. We hope this approach makes this book accessible to students, teachers, and teacher educators. The book includes appendices with sample activities related to each of the seven myths. We felt it was important to include these extended descriptions of activities along with their source texts because often teachers find great "raw material" but do not know how to transform it into a lesson. We recommend that each appendix be consulted after reading the corresponding chapter to better understand how the principles discussed apply to the sample activities. The activities can all be modified to include authentic texts from a wide variety of sources and for a wide variety of proficiency levels.

Throughout this book, we talk about both second and foreign language settings and both English and other languages. The language learning principles and accompanying research, such as how vocabulary is best learned and the importance of explicit instruction, apply equally to all languages and settings, both foreign language contexts (e.g., German instruction in the U.S., English instruction in Japan) as well as L2 contexts (e.g., English instruction in the U.S., French instruction in Quebec). The only exceptions, as discussed in the Epilogue, are related to learning how to read in character-based languages; some of the activities discussed throughout this book may indeed be more challenging for use in Chinese or Japanese classrooms. Generally, it is not so much the language being taught as it is the students' needs that will drive one's choice of authentic materials. ESL teachers, for example, will want to choose materials related to their students' daily lives or their academic needs. Teachers of foreign languages, including English teachers abroad, may choose materials that might be entertaining or that motivate and interest their students.

The majority of the research that we discuss is related to English, but some studies have also been conducted with learners of Spanish or French. The abundance of research on ESL learners is simply reflective of the field and does not imply that learning or teaching English is different than other languages, which is why we have included examples from French, German, and Spanish, as well as English, in the appendices. We hope that teachers of all languages can see these examples as templates for creating activities in any language.

MYTH **1**

Authentic texts are inaccessible to beginners.

In the Real World . . .

In my current position, I regularly observe graduate students who are teaching language courses for the first time. (This is Eve.) Recently, I had the opportunity to observe a Spanish instructor who was teaching accelerated first-quarter Spanish. Most of the students in the course were false beginners (i.e., they had some high school Spanish, but their knowledge of the language is too limited to place into a higher level). In addition to the false beginners, the class included true beginners— that is, students with no prior knowledge of the language. I visited the class during the fourth week of instruction; the theme of the chapter focused on food vocabulary and expressing likes and dislikes. We use a commercially produced textbook in the first-year program, but I encourage the instructors to incorporate authentic texts whenever possible.

On the day of my visit, the instructor reviewed food-related vocabulary and engaged the students in several communicative activities. Toward the end of class, he told the students they would watch a video. This video clip, which lasted approximately 35 seconds, was from a

13

cooking show in Latin America. The video was authentic and the native speaker (Chilean) spoke at a normal speed, including aspiration of the /s/ in the syllable-final position (*pescado* "fish" becomes [pe^{h}kado]. This phonological feature of Spanish can make it seem—to the non-native ear—that the speech is extremely fast. I observed the students as they watched the video for the first time, and their reaction was one that all language teachers are familiar with: the deer-in-the-headlights look. The students expressed disbelief at the speed of the video and wondered how they could be expected to understand it. I sat back and wondered how the instructor was going to salvage this part of his lesson plan. After the first viewing, the instructor reassured them that they would have several more opportunities to listen again, and he passed out a list of ten foods in Spanish. The students were to listen again and mark any of the food items mentioned by the native speaker. After the second viewing, most of the class had marked almost all of the items correctly. The instructor reviewed any unfamiliar vocabulary, which amounted to only one or two items. During the third viewing, their task was to put numbers next to the items, reflecting the order in which they were mentioned in the video. Again, most students were able to do this without difficulty. For the final viewing, the instructor played the video while projecting the corresponding transcript (in Spanish). Students read and listened at the same time. The lesson ended with some simple comprehension checks (e.g., *Is he a vegetarian?*) that all the students answered without hesitation. The deer-in-the-headlights look was gone, and students expressed satisfaction with how much they understood, which they estimated to be about 75 percent.

This is a story with a happy ending: An authentic text that seemed inaccessible initially was made accessible to students of Spanish in the fourth week of instruction. If we analyze the situation, we come to understand that several factors made the authentic text accessible. First, the content of the video dealt with a familiar subject matter (food preferences) and reinforced what the students had been learning in class. In addition, the length of the video (only 35 seconds) made it possible to work with multiple viewings. Finally, it is important to highlight the choice of task. Note that marking vocabulary words on a list does not require you to understand everything that is being said. In essence, students were being asked to recognize certain words in their aural form in a rapid stream of speech. Anecdotally, the fact that they were able to accomplish this task served as a motivational boost: They could understand a *real* native speaker talking about a *real* topic.

Unfortunately, I have also observed classroom situations in which authentic texts create a frustrating and ultimately unsuccessful learning experience. Authentic texts are difficult on many levels and, if not presented properly, students will become frustrated very quickly (this is especially true for beginners). But this is not reason enough to deprive beginners of authentic texts! The goal of this chapter is to persuade the reader that some authentic texts are accessible to beginners if presented properly and with adequate pedagogical support.

What the Research Says . . .

If authentic texts are beneficial for the numerous reasons presented in the introduction, then why are teachers sometimes reluctant to use them with beginning-level learners? Most likely the reluctance stems from the perceived difficulty of authentic texts. Indeed, authentic materials are likely to be difficult for beginners for a number of different reasons. Aural texts, such as the video example described in the beginning of this chapter, present a significant challenge because authentic speech is fast and full of reduced forms and, sometimes, colloquial language (Field, 2003). Written texts, especially authentic literary texts, can be very difficult because they lend themselves to multiple interpretations. Alvstad and Castro (2009), in arguing for the value of literary texts vis-à-vis other types of texts, remind us that "there are many ways of interpreting a text, and that these ways are historically situated and constrained" (p. 181). Likewise, Bernhardt (2002) affirms that literary texts "are inherently ambiguous, full of metaphor and intertextual relations to texts to which the readers have no access" (p. 198). Finally, vocabulary research has shown that a large vocabulary (8,000–9,000 word families) is needed to read authentic literary texts independently (Nation, 2006).

It is not our intent to dispute the inherent difficulty of authentic texts, and indeed, this is probably the source of the myth. Yet the research shows that learners of all proficiency levels, including beginners, can benefit from authentic texts. The empirical studies on this topic are all classroom-based—typically, one of the classes is exposed to authentic texts while the other follows the standard, textbook-based curriculum. The groups are then compared to one another in terms of their improvement on various measures (cf. Gilmore, 2011). In addition to these classroom-based studies, of which there are relatively few, there are numerous published articles that provide valuable suggestions for working with authentic texts with learners of all proficiency levels.

One of the earliest classroom-based studies to demonstrate the feasibility of working with authentic texts at the beginner level is Weyers (1999), who experimented with an authentic Mexican soap opera (*telenovela*) in two sections of a second-semester Spanish course. The rationale for using a *telenovela* was the familiarity of the genre for the students. Even if they were not avid consumers of American soap operas, the idea was that students would be able to "call on even their most superficial familiarity with the soap opera genre in predicting future events" (Weyers, 1999, p. 340). The study compared two groups that followed the same textbook curriculum, but the experimental group's activities were supplemented with 14 episodes of the *telenovela* (they watched two episodes per week during class time, which amounted to approximately 90 minutes of viewing time per week). It was hypothesized that the quantity and quality of the input provided by the *telenovela* would enhance the experimental group's acquisition of Spanish, specifically with respect to listening comprehension skills and oral proficiency. The results of the study were promising. In terms of listening comprehension (which was measured with a standardized test produced by the American Association of Teachers of Spanish and Portuguese), the experimental group improved significantly more than the control group. Oral proficiency was measured by means of a picture description task. Again, the experimental group outperformed the control group in terms of quantity of production (number of words-per-minute) and on two measures of quality: confidence in speech (defined as self-corrections and hesitations) and scope and breadth of response (defined as amount of detail provided for each picture).

In light of these favorable results, it is necessary to consider the kinds of tasks that accompanied the viewing of the *telenovela*. Weyers (1999) explains that task preparation included an advance organizer to help students understand the plot (i.e., written synopsis in English and description of the characters and their family history). In addition, a basic vocabulary list was provided for the first five episodes. Prior to viewing each episode, students reviewed a list of ten comprehension questions that would help them listen selectively for the main events. The comprehension questions were in Spanish, but students answered them in English. Finally, Weyers explains that the commercial breaks, which were fast-forwarded through during the viewing, served as short breaks that allowed the instructor to check for comprehension.

A similar classroom-based study is Maxim (2002), who compared two groups of true beginners in a first-semester German course. The experimental group read a 142-page authentic romance novel. The novel was in German but was originally translated from English. (Maxim maintains that a translation is authentic given the audience for whom it was written: native German speakers.) Students began reading the novel after the fourth week of instruction and read for a total of ten weeks. Crucially, the reading was a collaborative activity that took place in class for approximately 20 minutes daily. While the experimental group read the novel, the control group completed a variety of text-book activities designed to activate students' knowledge of specific grammar and vocabulary. In this sense, the experimental group was at a disadvantage because those students spent less time than the control group practicing grammar and vocabulary activities from the textbook. Despite this, there were no significant differences between the two groups on departmental exams, which suggests that reading the novel did not disadvantage the experimental group. Maxim also tested the learners' reading ability with a reading exam that targeted four different kinds of texts, but found no significant differences between the groups.

Although the quantitative results of Maxim (2002) might be considered disappointing (recall that there was no significant advantage on any of the assessment measures for the group that read an authentic novel), the study has important implications. Contrary to expectations, Maxim demonstrated that first-semester students—true beginners—were able to read an authentic novel despite their limited proficiency in German. Maxim attributes this to two aspects of the reading material: the cultural familiarity of the genre and the collaborative nature of the reading activity. In a related article, Maxim (2006) describes the pedagogical sequence of working with the romance novel in class. Pre-reading focused on activating students' background knowledge of the genre (e.g., themes typical in romance novels), anticipating the content based on the title, and setting realistic expectations for the reading comprehension process. This last step was vital in terms of orienting students to the idea that they could read without understanding every word on the page. The first stage of reading was guided by asking students to identify the major events and figures of the novel (i.e., the *who*, *where*, *when*, and *what*). The second stage of reading involved a worksheet that students completed with relevant details about people, their specific characteristics, and any resulting actions. Crucially, students were encouraged to use the actual language from the text to complete the worksheet rather than to produce original language. After reading a chapter during class, students were asked to write a one-paragraph summary in German, again using five different phrases or expressions directly from the chapter. Maxim (2006) highlights the importance of "recycling textual language" (p. 27) in order to compensate for learners' limited proficiency.

If we consider the studies by Weyers (1999) and Maxim (2002) as successful cases of making authentic texts accessible to beginners, we note many similarities between the types of text used in both studies. The genre (romance novel/soap opera) was considered culturally familiar to the learners. In other words, learners were assumed to have the appropriate cultural schema (Oller, 1995) for understanding the texts, which means that the sociocultural situations in the texts are not totally foreign to the reader/viewer and, as a result, the learner has the advantage of being able to identify with the characters and generate the right expectations. A number of studies have demonstrated the positive effects of cultural familiarity on reading comprehension (Alptekin, 2006; Carrell, 1987; Erten & Razi, 2009; Steffensen, Joag-Dev, & Anderson, 1979). Furthermore, the learners likely already possessed a relevant formal schema that facilitated their understanding of the text. Formal schema (see also Myth 4) refers to knowledge of how texts are typically organized as well as the main features of a genre. For example, Latin American *telenovelas* almost always involve an impossible romance (e.g., a woman in love with a man from a much higher social class) that ultimately gets resolved at the end despite numerous obstacles and tensions along the way. So despite not being familiar with the specific situation of the protagonists in a particular soap opera, knowledge of the formal schema allows learners to make reasonable assumptions about the development of the plot. Moreover, soap operas/romance novels are rhetorically organized in such a way that facilitates comprehension. Alptekin and Erçetin (2011) explain that a coherent narrative with a well-developed storyline demands less attentional resources than other types of texts, specifically expository texts. On this view, narrative texts are "easier to process because they have a close correspondence to daily events in contextually specific situations" (Alptekin & Erçetin, 2011, p. 244).

In addition to their conventional rhetorical organization, soap operas and romance novels feature a great deal of repetition. Weyers (1999) argued that the *telenovela* "offers continuity" (p. 339) because each episode builds on prior events. In fact, each episode of a *telenovela* begins with a brief (two- or three-minute) review of the previous episode for the viewers that may have missed a day's programming. This continuity is precisely what Rodgers and Webb (2011) appeal to when recommending that L2 learners watch successive episodes of a single TV program, since "cumulative gains in background knowledge" (p. 705) will likely increase their comprehension of subsequent episodes. Along similar lines, Maxim (2006) mentions the redundancy of the romance novel, which provides learners "the opportunity to become familiar with the characters, their behavior, the locations, and the language used to characterize these recurring images" (p. 23). Another similarity between the studies is the use of relatively long narratives. The students in Weyers' study watched 14 episodes of the *telenovela*, totaling more than ten hours of viewing. In Maxim's study the students read a 142-page novel containing approximately 40,000 words. Maxim notes that longer texts might actually be easier for beginners because of the forementioned continuity and redundancy (see Myth 3 for a discussion of this issue).

An essential element of the pedagogical approach described in both Weyers (1999) and Maxim (2002, 2006) is the fact that learners were not asked to read or view the material independently. Both studies included significant instructor support. Since learners viewed the *telenovela* and read the romance novel in class, they were able to clear up any misunderstandings "on the spot" and request assistance with linguistic difficulties. In both studies, students' reading/viewing was supported with a variety of level-appropriate tasks that served to enhance their comprehension of the texts. We will revisit the issue of level-appropriate tasks in the *What We Can Do* section at the end of this chapter.

In addition to classroom-based studies such as Weyers (1999) and Maxim (2002), many scholarly articles describe procedures or best practices for using certain types of authentic texts with beginners. These studies, however, do not involve comparisons between groups and thus cannot provide clear evidence that authentic texts are superior to some other type of materials. Nevertheless, these studies are grounded in the experience of the researchers, who presumably have experimented with the texts in their own classrooms. For example, Barrette, Paesani, and Vinall (2010) presented a sample lesson plan for working with the short story *Apocalipsis* (by Argentine author Marcos Denevi) at beginning, intermediate, and advanced levels. The authors chose *Apocalipsis* because of its thematic familiarity to students. It is a story about the disappearance of the human race that touches on the theme of technology and its potentially destructive effects. Barrette et al. maintain that this text can be used with beginners provided that it is accompanied by level-appropriate tasks. For example, they propose that teachers focus on familiar information and link the story to students' personal experiences. To facilitate comprehension, the authors suggest that teachers provide students with an unordered list of the main events in the story (this list can include vocabulary directly from the story to pre-teach difficult words). Students can be asked to predict the order of events as a pre-reading activity and verify their predictions (during or after reading). Additional pedagogical articles similar to Barrette et al. (2010) are given in Table 1.1, with details regarding the type of text and target audience.

All of the articles listed in Table 1.1 specifically target beginning-level learners. More research is available on exploiting authentic texts in intermediate- and advanced-level courses. For example, Bridges (2009) illustrated how to work with a graphic novel in a third-year German course, and Bueno (2009) provided concrete examples of incorporating film into an advanced Spanish conversation and composition course. Since this chapter focuses on learners at the beginner level, we do not discuss these articles further, but we note that many of the ideas may be applicable to lower-level courses.

Table 1.1: Best Practices for Using Authentic Texts with Beginners

Article	Target Language and Type of Text	Pedagogical Approach
Katz (2001)	French; literary texts (poem and short story)	Structured input and output activities
Davidheiser (2007)	German; fairy tales adapted for beginners (i.e., shortened and updated with modern vocabulary)	Focus on oral retellings of the fairy tales; ideas for working with the grammar in the texts are also provided.
Adair-Hauck & Donato (2002)	French; francophone folktales	PACE model: an inductive approach to grammar teaching using storytelling
Redmann (2008)	German; *Emil und die Detektive* (a well-known children's novel)	A comprehensive approach to teaching the novel, including a reading journal, grammar, and vocabulary activities.

Another feasible option for having beginners work with authentic texts is an approach known as *narrow reading*. Narrow reading involves reading a series of texts on the same topic (Kang, 2015; Krashen, 2004; Schmitt & Carter, 2000). For example, learners might read a series of newspaper articles pertaining to a particular cultural issue or political event. By reading on the same topic (e.g., the political crisis in Venezuela), learners will naturally encounter the same vocabulary items more than once. Schmitt and Carter (2000) demonstrated this by comparing two sets of news stories: one on a related topic (the death of Princess Diana) and a set of unrelated stories from the same newspaper. They analyzed the vocabulary within these texts and found that high-frequency content words occurred much more often in the related set of stories than in the random set. For example, words like *death, palace, royal, crash,* and *photographers* were repeated in the Diana news stories; this repetition is hypothesized to play an important role in improving comprehension as well as the likelihood of learning these words. By lowering the vocabulary load placed on the learner, Schmitt and Carter maintain that "narrow reading can facilitate the transition to these [authentic] texts, and perhaps permit earlier access to them" (p. 8). Schmitt and Carter also provided practical advice for incorporating narrow reading into the syllabus, such as polling students for their preferences in order to choose a story or topic that will pique their interest. Alternatively, narrow reading can become a highly individualized feature of the course if students are given the autonomy to choose their own topics and then produce an assignment based on what they have read (e.g., a summary, a contextualized vocabulary list).

What We Can Do . . .

1. Realize that it's possible to incorporate authentic texts without necessarily restructuring the curriculum.

In Weyers (1999) and Maxim (2002), the authentic texts supplemented the standard curriculum; they did not replace it. Others (Allen & Paesani, 2010; Barrette et al., 2010; Swaffar & Arens, 2005) have argued for a complete restructuring of the curriculum in order to alleviate problems associated with the language-literature split that characterizes the dominant paradigm for foreign language teaching in the United States. However, restructuring the curriculum may be a daunting prospect and is often beyond the control of most individual teachers. In light of this situation, remember that authentic texts can be used to enhance an already-existing curriculum that revolves around a textbook. For example, the scenario described at the beginning of this chapter illustrated how a listening comprehension activity (based on an authentic text) was brought in to reinforce and enhance the textbook presentation of food vocabulary.

2. Select the materials very carefully.

Some of the criteria you will want to consider include length, topic familiarity, text structure, and the linguistic complexity of the text.

- **Length:** There is no simple answer to the issue of length, which we discuss in detail in Myth 3. When working with beginners, the key observation is that lengthier texts will need to be divided up into smaller segments. For example, viewing a feature film that uses the L2 in one sitting will be overwhelming for the beginner and does not give you much opportunity to monitor comprehension during viewing. Consider using a scene from a film for a specific purpose (e.g., to enhance a theme-based unit on marriage customs or illustrate a speech act such as leave-taking or greeting). If you want to work with the entire film, realize that you will need to break it up into viewable chunks (e.g., ten-minute segments).

- **Topic familiarity:** Consider how much your students know about the topic (the less they know, the more "foreign" the material will be, and thus, more difficult) and how familiar they are with the genre. Although you can do a lot of pre-viewing (in the case of film) and pre-reading (in the case of written text), consider the time investment. Do you want to do two hours of pre-reading so that your students can read a two-paragraph news report?

- **Text structure:** There are various ways of arranging ideas in a text, which can vary across genres and disciplines. For example, flashbacks in literature and non-chronological presentation of events in historical texts are quite common. With beginners, it is probably best to limit yourself to texts that have a conventional narrative structure. You can anticipate that flashbacks and unconventional narrative structures will likely confuse the beginning-level learner.

- **Linguistic complexity of the text:** This criterion is probably what most teachers intuitively look for when selecting authentic texts. Texts with challenging vocabulary and long, complex sentences can be considered complex in a quantitative sense, although there are clearly other dimensions of text complexity. There is ongoing academic debate as to what makes a text complex, especially in relation to the Common Core State Standards in the United States and the needs of English language learners (cf., Bunch, Walqui, & Pearson, 2014; Wong Fillmore, 2014). When working with beginners, our recommendation is to select materials in which at least some of the vocabulary will be familiar to your students (see the anecdote at the beginning of this chapter). Not only will this make the text more accessible, but it provides repeated exposure to the vocabulary they are learning, thus allowing them to consolidate knowledge of newly or partially learned words.

3. Choose level-appropriate tasks.

This is probably the most important recommendation when working with authentic texts.

Swaffar and Arens (2005, p. 61) [as cited in Barrette et al., 2010] maintain that "there is scarcely a right or wrong text for a particular learning level, but there are definitely right or wrong tasks." Perhaps the key point here is that learners do not have to understand everything in order to get something out of a particular text. Indeed, it is important to remind your students of this as you approach a text for the first time. The success or failure of working with authentic materials, especially with beginners, will depend on the teacher's ability to create the right kind of task. An extreme example of a wrong task would be to have beginning-level learners transcribe an audio clip. Table 1.2 provides some examples of appropriate tasks for beginners and where these are illustrated in the research.

Table 1.2: Appropriate Tasks for Beginners

Type of Task Suitable to Beginners	Research Support
Attention to major events (who, what, when, where)	Maxim (2006)
Order events in chronological order	Barrette et al. (2010)
Collaborative reading	Maxim (2002; 2006)
Binary options (agree/disagree); matching	Katz (2002)
Worksheet partially filled-in by the teacher (e.g., people, their characteristics, and resulting actions)	Maxim (2006)
Comprehension questions as advance organizer; answer in L1	Weyers (1999)

4. Consider working with authentic materials that are not text-laden.

Examples of these types of materials are charts, brochures, greeting cards, and schedules. Especially useful are information graphics (i.e., infographics) that provide clear visual representations of data. For example, I recently came across a published infographic that showed the basic school supplies (and their total cost) required for Mexican students in public schools. An infographic such as this is visually appealing and not intimidating for a beginning learner; it could be used as early as the second week of first-semester Spanish when students learn basic vocabulary about the classroom. Similarly, I recently observed a beginning-level class in which the instructor showed a Spanish language greeting card that she had received from a relative. It was an excellent supplement that not only introduced students to a kinship term (*madrina* "godmother") but also to the cultural significance behind the term. Of course, finding the right authentic material for your students is just the first step. See Appendix A for ideas on creating interesting tasks that are appropriate for beginners.

Authentic texts cannot
be used to teach grammar.

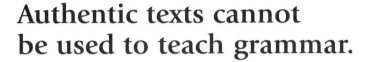

In the Real World . . .

When I first began teaching at UC, Santa Cruz, I was assigned to teach an intermediate Spanish language course. (This is Eve.) The textbook we were using was new to me, so I made a conscious effort to include most of the material, simply to get a feel for the progression of the activities and how much time to devote to each chapter. One of the chapters had a grammatical focus on past tense forms (the preterit and imperfect in Spanish) and how to use both in combination in past tense narrations. Those who have learned or taught Spanish will agree that the preterit/imperfect contrast is one of the classic problems for L2 learners since the distinction depends on many factors, including how the speaker chooses to frame a particular event or state. To give just one example, the phrase *I was afraid* can be expressed with either preterit (*Tuve miedo*) or the imperfect (*Tenía miedo*) depending on context.

Thus, as we worked through this particular textbook chapter, I gave students many opportunities to narrate in the past, both in class and for homework. We did all the grammar activities in the textbook in addition to original ones I had created. The chapter concluded with an authentic literary text: a short story by the renowned Mexican poet and author José Emilio Pacheco ("Aqueronte"). It's an interesting read with an enigmatic ending that lends itself to multiple interpretations. Notwithstanding its literary value, the entire story is told in the present tense. For example, it begins with *Son las cinco de la tarde* ("It is five o'clock") . . . *la muchacha entra en el café* ("the girl enters the café"), and so on. After reading and discussing the story, one of my students asked me point blank: "Why is this story in the present tense when all we've been doing for the last two weeks is working on the preterit and imperfect?" Indeed, this was a perceptive student who was asking a relevant question. And worse yet, I had no good answer. Why had the textbook publishers chosen this particular short story instead of one that situated events in the past, which would have been ideal for highlighting the use of preterit and imperfect in a discourse context?

I suspect that the short story "Aqueronte" was chosen not for its grammatical characteristics but rather for its thematic value and the chapter's cultural focus on Mexico. But this leads to further questioning about how authentic texts are utilized in textbooks and language classrooms: texts are typically chosen for their inherent (often literary) value, while grammar is taught separately, with descriptions and rules aimed at accuracy at the sentence level. In fact, when I reviewed the grammar explanations in that textbook, I confirmed that the examples were mostly contrived sentences and a couple of short, scripted paragraphs. In other words, it was clear to me that grammar and authentic texts in this textbook (any many others just like it) don't mix. Conversely, I had also realized that any language focus that was provided to support learners to use the authentic text was generally in the form of vocabulary in the pre-reading section.

In this chapter we will argue that authentic texts can be exploited effectively to teach grammar. In order to achieve this, however, we have to share an understanding of grammar as more than forms, but rather as form-meaning relationships that exist at the discourse level. A case in point is the example of *tuve miedo* (preterit) versus *tenía miedo* (imperfect) mentioned previously. Both are grammatical, but the decision to use one over the other cannot be made at the sentence level. It is actually the surrounding discourse that determines whether the intended meaning is change of state (*tuve miedo*) or an emotional state that sets the scene (*tenía miedo*). Furthermore, 'teaching grammar' must be understood broadly to include "any instructional technique that draws learners' attention to some specific grammatical form" (Ellis, 2006, p. 84). As we will see in this chapter, authentic texts are particularly well suited to an inductive approach in which learners are led to discover certain grammatical generalizations based on examples found in the input from the source text. This is contrasted in Myth 4 with examples of a more deductive approach that might be needed to prepare students for difficult structures they may encounter in a text.

What the Research Says . . .

My experience with that particular Spanish textbook, reiterated by the insightful student who noticed the disconnect between the grammar we were studying and the authentic text in the chapter, is not uncommon. Fernández (2011) analyzed the approach to grammar instruction in six Spanish textbooks that are routinely used at the university level. Her analysis, which focused on those chapters in which the preterit was introduced, examined the type of explicit information provided, the samples of language that were used to illustrate the grammar point, and the types of activities. Not surprisingly, none of the textbooks provided language from authentic sources in the grammar sections; all data were in the form of contrived (or invented) sources (both discrete sentences and brief paragraphs) or through captioned illustrations. Crucially, Fernández is not claiming that these textbooks do not contain authentic material; her analysis demonstrates that authentic texts are not typically used for the purpose of illustrating or teaching grammatical structures.

There are at least three reasons why authentic materials do not mesh well with textbook grammar presentations. First, it is likely that textbooks reflect a view of grammar as knowledge of rules that account for accurate language at the sentence level. As Richards and Reppen (2014) explain, in traditional approaches to grammar instruction, the unit of focus is the sentence; students are given the opportunity to practice the target item in order to produce correct sentences. Yet, as we know, the ability to use grammar correctly and appropriately in communicative contexts goes far beyond the sentence level. This view of grammar, which underscores the fact that grammar is about choices (for example, we choose the passive or active voice depending on how much we want to focus on the agent), situates grammar at the level of the text. According to Larsen-Freeman (2003), a text is "any stretch of language that functions as a whole unit" (p. 67). In contrast to the traditional sentence-level approach, a view of grammar at the level of text requires us to consider how grammatical forms work in discourse and recognizes that "the grammatical system offers its users choices in how they wish to realize meanings and position themselves ideologically and socially" (Larsen-Freeman, 2015, p. 272). This view complements and broadens our understanding of grammar at the sentence-level. It is not difficult to think of examples of grammatical structures that must be appreciated at the discourse level (consider the English article system or the preterit/imperfect contrast in Romance languages).

In addition to its focus on the sentence-level, traditional approaches to grammar teaching tend to prioritize one dimension of grammar—form. For example, in learning the passive voice, textbook exercises may ask learners to transform active sentences into passive ones. Additional grammar exercises that most language teachers are probably familiar with include conjugating verbs to fill in the blanks, replacing noun phrases with pronouns, and constructing sentences out of a series of given elements. However, as proposed by Larsen-Freeman (2003), we can better understand grammar in terms of three dimensions: *form* (how is it formed?) *meaning* (what does it mean?), and *use* (when is it used versus another form that expresses a similar meaning?). Larsen-Freeman emphasizes that it is not always form that poses the greatest learning challenge for L2 learners. Instead, many difficulties in grammar lie in the use dimension, which requires speakers to make choices depending on context, one's intended meaning, and

Figure 2.1: The Three Dimensions of the Spanish Present Perfect

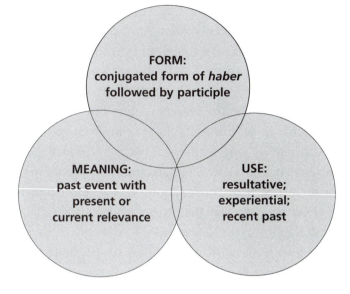

pragmatic considerations. Of course, there are grammatical structures that are morphologically or syntactically complex and thus pose a form problem. The form dimension cannot be ignored, but a complete picture of grammar comes into view only when we consider form in conjunction with meaning and use. To better appreciate the three dimensions of grammar, consider the Spanish present perfect, which is similar—but not identical—to the English present perfect (e.g., *have arrived, has seen*), as shown in Figure 2.1.

When the present perfect is introduced in Spanish textbooks, the emphasis is generally on the form dimension, presumably because there are several irregular participle forms that must be memorized. The meaning of the present perfect is presented with English equivalents and is assumed to be relatively straightforward. The use dimension, however, tends to be neglected. In understanding the use dimension, we must clarify when the present perfect is preferred over a form with a similar meaning such as the preterit. Specifically, in what contexts would a speaker choose *he visto* ("I have seen") versus *vi* ("I saw")? The use dimension would also address the fact that Spanish present perfect is not used for events that started in the past and continue in the present, unlike in English (e.g., *I have lived here for ten years*). In a more advanced course, the use dimension might also address regional variation—it is well known that present perfect usage varies considerably between Latin America and Spain. In sum, textbooks and traditional grammar materials are oriented toward asking learners to correctly form the present perfect, but at the same time they tend to overlook the learning challenge of appropriate use.

The third reason why textbooks and other pedagogical materials favor contrived sentences to illustrate grammar points has to do with convenience. As noted by Cook (2001), it is generally quicker and easier to use invented examples than to search for authentic ones that are pedagogically appropriate. Related to the convenience factor, it is clear that contrived texts allow for many instances of the same structure or form. In other words, it is easy to seed the language sample with relative pronouns, reflexive verbs, the accusative case, or any other grammar point that needs to be illustrated. For example, a quick glance at a first-year Spanish textbook shows how relative pronouns are illustrated with a contrived text about Cuzco, Perú. The short paragraph (less than 150 words) contains ten examples of relative pronouns, both with and without prepositions [e.g., *que* ("that"), *en la que* ("in which"), *donde* ("where"), *a la que* ("to which"), *del que* ("of which")]. Presumably it would be very difficult to find an authentic text of this length with so many instances of relative pronouns. Authentic texts are generally more varied in terms of lexis and grammar because they were written with a communicative purpose rather than to illustrate a particular language form. In contrast, contrived texts written for pedagogical purposes often contain the target grammatical form in unnatural proportions.

A final point that deserves mention here is that teaching grammar via authentic texts requires us to consider how grammar and vocabulary are interrelated. Although traditionally grammar and vocabulary are taught (and presented in textbooks) as two separate domains, the reality is that the two are inherently connected, leading some researchers to use the term *lexicogrammar* (cf. Liu & Jiang, 2009). One example of this is that knowing how to use a word correctly involves some degree of grammatical knowledge, such as knowing its part of speech and what other words it can appear with (collocations). Consider the word *diet*: learners of English might learn the basic meaning of this word and yet still use it incorrectly if they don't know the common phrases *to go on a diet* or *to be on a diet*. Many corpus studies, which are reviewed later in this chapter, are designed to engage learners in noticing the typical patterns in which particular words are used. Thus, by including attention to nuances of meaning and collocation patterns, the focus of grammar instruction is necessarily much broader than in a traditional approach. The rest of this chapter is organized according to the two main strands of research that use authentic texts to teach grammar (in the broad sense previously described).

Literary Approaches

There is a growing body of research that argues in favor of using literature as a source of comprehensible input to "demonstrate appropriate uses of particular grammatical rules as well as how grammar conveys meaning" (Frantzen, 2013, p. 628). This section examines several pedagogical proposals that share certain elements, most notably the use of literary texts as a vehicle for inductive grammar presentation.

Paesani (2005) proposes combining an inductive approach to grammar and interactive reading instruction. She illustrates this with a lesson for beginning-level French that targets the relative pronouns *que* and *où*. The central ingredient of the lesson is a well-known poem by Prévert entitled *Le Message* ("The Message"), which is highly repetitive in its use of the aforementioned relative pronouns (cf. Katz, 2001, for a structured input approach to a different Prévert poem). The lesson begins with a number of pre-reading activities that serve to activate students' schemata and essential vocabulary. After reading the poem and demonstrating comprehension, the lesson shifts to a focus on form— in this case the relative pronouns that appear in each line of the poem. Students underline all examples of relative pronouns in the text and then propose a rule for the use of *que* (direct object relative) versus *où* (locative relative). The lesson continues with more targeted grammar practice as well as post-reading activities that explore the poem's content and themes.

In order to successfully implement the sequence proposed by Paesani (2005), two comments are in order. First, the chosen text is used initially as comprehensible input; this means that students must demonstrate basic understanding of the text and engage with it as meaningful content before the grammar focus of the lesson. Second, the choice of text is crucial in that it must have sufficient exemplars of the target form or structure. In Paesani's sample lesson, the short poem is replete with relative pronouns (every line contains either *que* or *où*), making it what has been called an *input flood*. Note that most authentic texts will not be so repetitive and may have fewer instances of the given grammatical form.

Mojica-Díaz and Sánchez-López (2010) outline a similar proposal for teaching the Spanish preterit/imperfect, although their approach is geared towards advanced learners. Grammar is taught inductively through the initial presentation of a literary text, although the authors explain that other genres of authentic text might also be used (e.g., journalistic articles, songs, film reviews). The lesson plan proceeds in a way that resembles that of Paesani (2005). Students first read the text for meaning and answer comprehension questions. Next, they engage in a grammatical analysis that begins with underlining all the verbs in the text; after establishing that the story is narrated in the past, the students highlight the sentences in the preterit and the imperfect. Working in groups, they discuss why the author used either the preterit or the imperfect in the given context. They fill in a chart with the attested examples and the reasons behind preterit and imperfect usage. Finally, they apply their findings to a new text (another short story) with the goal of refining their initial hypotheses. It is only at the end of the pedagogical sequence that the instructor assumes a more active role, making revisions or corrections to the students' chart. Mojica-Díaz and Sánchez-López believe that the benefit of this approach, which they refer to as 'discovery-based' learning, is that it ". . . allows the learner to be actively involved in the process by forming and testing hypotheses concerning the function and meaning of grammatical structures in a given context" (p. 483).

The approach to teaching grammar described by Mojica-Díaz and Sánchez-López (2010) is certainly well-suited to a group of advanced learners who will appreciate seeing how the preterit and imperfect are interwoven in narrative contexts. Nevertheless, there are some potential pitfalls as well. In particular, the approach is very much focused on reasons that underlie usage. Reasons can be very difficult to articulate since they are broader than rules (Larsen-Freeman, 2003). In the specific case of the preterit/imperfect, the choice of form conveys subtle shifts in perspective that may be very difficult for L2 learners (even near-native speakers!) to perceive (see Frantzen, 2013, for excellent examples). To guide the students during the inductive grammar phase of the lesson, an alternative would be to provide them with three or four known functions of the preterit and imperfect (e.g., the imperfect for habitual actions) and let them identify the instances in the text that exemplify those particular functions.

Another study worthy of mention here is Kingsbury (2011), which provides an exhaustive analysis of how to focus on grammar using Marco Deveni's novel *Rosaura a las diez*. This well-known detective novel is commonly used in intermediate/advanced Spanish courses. Kingsbury explains how the novel can be exploited for grammatical analysis, leading the students to notice how particular linguistic choices create meaning and establish relationships among the characters. Since it is a longer text, there are numerous options for focusing on Spanish grammar, including various verb forms (e.g., preterit/ imperfect, the subjunctive, the future of probability), forms of address (formal and informal), and diminutive suffixes. Kingsbury proposes specific grammar activities, such as taking an extract from the text and changing the verbs into the infinitive; students determine if the preterit or imperfect would go better in each context, with the final step a comparison of their answers with the original rendition.

As an interim conclusion to this section, we must point out that authentic (literary) texts were the cornerstone of teaching in traditional methods such as grammar-translation. None of the studies surveyed here are advocating a return to grammar-translation pedagogy. Instead, they address the important question of how to provide a discourse context for understanding the meanings conveyed by particular grammatical forms. Literary works provide a rich context for grammar teaching, but the text itself is the raw material: it is up to the teacher to design activities based on the text that will allow learners to actively work with the grammar contained therein (see Appendix B for examples).

Corpus-Based Approaches

In recent years, corpora and corpus tools have had a major impact on research in linguistics and applied linguistics. In contrast, corpus-based applications in L2 pedagogy are somewhat less mainstream due to a gap between research and practice (cf. Römer, 2011; Reinhardt, 2010). Instead of examining the possible reasons why corpus-based pedagogy has not been implemented in most ESL/L2 classrooms, we focus instead on concrete examples of research that utilize corpora to enhance grammar teaching.

A corpus can be loosely defined as any collection of spoken or written language, but more precisely, corpora are huge repositories of language that are stored electronically and allow the user to search for particular items. With respect to English, well-known examples are the British National Corpus (BNC), the Corpus of Contemporary American English (COCA), and the Michigan Corpus of Academic Spoken English (MICASE). There are corpora for other languages, including Spanish (e.g., *Corpus de Referencia del Español Actual*), Portuguese (e.g., *Corpus do Português*), and German (e.g., Leipzig/BYU Corpus of Contemporary German), to name just a few.

Language data extracted from corpora are by definition authentic since they are collections of native speaker usage (there are also learner corpora, which would fall into a different category). The potential benefit of corpus-based pedagogy is the ability to expose learners to real language use in context, although the notion of *context* must be examined critically (see discussion at the end of this section), thereby facilitating awareness of language patterns. To give a simple example, the question "What prepositions go with a particular verb?" can be easily answered with a corpus search, providing hundreds of examples. Search data often comes in the form of concordance lines, which highlight the key word and provide a specified number of words to the left and to the right (this is known as the *key word in context* or KWIC format). For example, a search for the keyword *squander* in COCA, limited to the spoken register, yields 59 tokens, including the following:

1. exaggerated the threat to the United States causing the U.S. to **squander** hundreds of millions of dollars in unnecessary military

2. chunks of our hard-earned income to the federal government to **squander** as it sees fit

3. get a check at the beginning of the month which they **squander** the first two weeks

A glance at the concordance data will give the user a good sense of how this verb is used in English, specifically the kinds of nouns that generally appear with it. When reading these concordance lines, the user is engaged in what Gabrielatos (2005) calls "condensed reading" (p. 9), which shares features of intensive and extensive reading. It is intensive in the sense that learners are focusing on the behavior of a specific language form (e.g., *squander* in the examples above), but at the same time it is extensive because learners are exposed to a large number of examples, many more than would be provided in a typical dictionary entry. In addition, Gabrielatos points out that a corpus search can provide not only a larger number of examples but also more variety within the examples (i.e., different collocations) than a single authentic text.

The types of research that we examine in this section can be grouped under the category of direct corpus applications (Römer, 2011) in the sense that teachers and/or learners are interacting directly with corpus data. Furthermore, all of the studies are representative of data-driven learning (DDL). Pioneered by Johns (1994), DDL is fundamentally an inductive approach to learning that involves the student in the discovery of language patterns. In the strict interpretation of DDL, the learner interacts directly with the corpus to discover patterns or solve specific problems. However, some have cautioned that giving learners total autonomy with corpus searches may not always yield positive results. Even when learners are trained to use a corpus, research has shown that they often feel overwhelmed by the extremely large number of examples generated (cf. Liu & Jiang, 2009) and too many unknown vocabulary items in the results. Alternatively, the teacher can interact with the corpus, select relevant samples, and then prepare materials or tasks for the students. In this way, teacher-prepared materials can reduce the burden for students and solve a number of practical problems associated with corpus-based pedagogy (cf. Boulton, 2010). Smart (2014) maintains that teacher-prepared materials do not compromise the spirit of DDL, which he sees as having two essential characteristics:

1. real language data as sources of language learning materials or reference resources

2. student-centered learning activities that focus on language discovery (p. 186)

The studies reviewed in this section all involve DDL as defined by Smart, either by having the students access the corpus directly or via carefully-designed teacher materials.

Liu and Jiang (2009) experimented with a corpus-based approach to teach English grammar in the ESL/English as a foreign language (EFL) context. The instructors who participated in the study underwent detailed, hands-on training in using corpus tools and designing sample classroom activities. The learners were all first language (L1) Chinese speakers with intermediate to upper-intermediate English language proficiency; they had direct access to the corpora (BNC and the BNC Baby) in order to perform searches related to various aspects of English lexicogrammar. For example, the students used concordance data to understand the difference in meaning and usage between the adjectives *uninterested* and *disinterested.* Another activity involved students in correcting their own errors on a composition, using the corpus as a resource. Liu and Jiang analyzed the students' work, instructors' teaching logs, and students' and instructors' post-study questionnaires to determine the effectiveness of the corpus-based approach. Although not all the learners were equally enthusiastic about corpus-based methods, the authors highlight the following positive trends: enhanced language awareness, a better command of lexicogrammatical rules and patterns, and a greater appreciation of the importance of context. There were benefits for the instructors as well: many of the teachers commented that they found the corpus useful for showing differences in usage without having to come up with fabricated examples on the spot (cf. Lin & Lee, 2015 for additional comments regarding teachers' perceptions of corpus-based pedagogy). In sum, the study by Liu and Jiang suggests that working with authentic language samples from a corpus search may be an effective teaching tool, especially in promoting discovery learning.

A more recent study by Benavides (2015) in the context of a Spanish grammar class replicated the hands-on approach of Liu and Jiang (2009). Students were trained to perform searches using the *Corpus del Español* (Davies, 2002) in order to enhance their understanding of grammatical concepts such as the preterit/imperfect contrast and the copular verbs *ser* and *estar*. The researcher provided students with both inductive and deductive assignments that required them to use the corpus to find examples that confirmed or contradicted the explanations in the textbook. The inductive exercises asked students to form a rule based on attested examples; the deductive exercises provided students with a rule (e.g., the imperfect is used for actions in progress) and asked them to find examples to support it. Interestingly, students' perceptions of the corpus-based activities were not overwhelmingly positive as shown in the results of a quantitative survey (mean score of 2.56 on a 5-point scale), yet their responses to open-ended questions revealed more positive comments. Benavides concludes that students were clearly engaged in DDL and that the corpus can be utilized effectively as a supplement or extension of the textbook.

The studies of Liu and Jiang (2009) and Benavides (2015) measured students' perceptions and attitudes toward the corpus-based approach rather than learning outcomes per se (i.e., as measured by gains on a test). Some empirical research is beginning to appear, such as a recent study by Smart (2014), which reveals that a combination of real language samples (extracted from a corpus) and inductive learning techniques are particularly successful in promoting grammar learning. Three groups of learners enrolled in an intensive English program in the U.S. studied the passive voice under different conditions. The first group (DDL) worked with paper-based materials that included concordance lines taken from various corpora. They were guided in the inductive approach—that is, by answering specific questions based on the examples. For example, they had to circle the subject of the sentences and then think about who was performing the action of the verb. The second group worked with the same corpus-based materials, but in a deductive approach that followed the traditional presentation-practice-production (PPP) sequence. The third group served as a control group, which received traditional PPP instruction based on a grammar textbook, not corpus-based language samples. The results reveal a significant advantage for the DDL group: they increased their mean score from the pre-test to the post-test and retained this gain on the delayed post-test. In contrast, the other groups did not show significant improvement over time. Smart maintains that the DDL group "engaged with the language learning activities and sample language in ways that the other groups did not" (p. 196), suggesting that they took a more active role because of the problem-solving nature of DDL.

Although DDL is particularly well-suited to advanced learners, Boulton (2010) showed that intermediate-level learners can also benefit from corpus-based materials that are prepared ahead of time by the teacher. A group of L1 French speakers in the EFL context participated in the study, which targeted ten problematic language forms (e.g., the difference between *only, alone, lone,* and *lonely*). Half of the forms were taught using traditional dictionary materials and the other half were taught with corpus-based materials. In other words, instead of comparing two groups of learners as Smart (2014) did, Boulton compared how well learners fared on items taught with one method versus another. The results indicate that both types of treatment had a significant effect, but there was no significant difference between the two treatments. Despite this, students perceived the corpus-based materials more favorably than the traditional materials, as one student noted that corpora helped with "[things] you don't find in a dictionary" (p. 554).

Many corpus researchers are interested in spoken grammar, which can be defined as "the manifestation of systematic grammatical phenomena in spoken discourse" (Cullen & Kuo, 2007, p. 363). In other words, it is the grammar that characterizes informal, conversational exchanges. A large body of research, especially for English, has shown that there are unique features of spoken grammar that are infrequent in written language; likewise, some grammatical forms, although present in both spoken and written registers, take on a different function in conversation. For example, the past progressive tense is widely used in conversations to introduce reported speech (e.g., *He* **was saying** *that real-estate is booming now*) (Biber et al., 1999; McCarthy & Carter, 2002, among others). Many scholars have argued that spoken grammar should have a more prominent role in language teaching (see Carter & McCarthy, in press, for a recent overview) and some of this research has found its way into ESL/EFL teaching materials, although there exists a good deal of variation among textbooks and the extent to which they incorporate features of spoken grammar (Cullen & Kuo, 2007).

Spoken grammar and authentic texts are a natural combination. In other words, authentic texts that are based on conversations (e.g., interviews, scenes from films) can be exploited for teaching features of spoken grammar. Timmis (2005) provides an excellent pedagogical model for teaching spoken grammar, based partially on the illustration-interaction-induction sequence proposed by McCarthy and Carter (1995). Timmis designed materials to accompany a BBC video series called "People and Places," which features native speakers talking about issues of local interest. The pedagogical sequence begins with pre-listening tasks that activate relevant background knowledge (Timmis labels these *cultural access tasks*). Next, learners listen to the text for meaning and answer global comprehension questions. Afterwards, learners engage in a number of noticing tasks that encourage them to compare their expectations of native-speaker English with the reality. The lesson ends with language discussion tasks that ask learners to reflect on why speakers used certain forms and the contexts in which it would be appropriate to use them. It must be noted that this approach for teaching spoken grammar does not actually require the learners to produce features of conversational English or imitate the native-speaker model; the focus is on noticing, enhanced awareness, and reflection pertaining to sociolinguistic concerns. Timmis emphasizes that authentic spoken texts should be listened to whenever possible, even if a written transcript of the text is available.

Barbieri and Eckhardt (2007) developed a pedagogical framework for teaching reported speech (e.g., *Alex said that he liked his new books.*) across written and spoken registers of English based on examples from corpora. The authors propose various consciousness-raising tasks, which are designed to help students "develop awareness at the level of understanding" (Barbieri & Eckhardt, p. 334). The tasks lead students through a series of steps such as reading the examples and identifying reporting verbs (e.g., *say, tell*); identifying the tense of the verb in the reported speech clause; rating the conversations in terms of formality, tone, age of speakers, and so on. Crucially, the language samples are provided to the students (i.e., students are not directly interacting with the corpus). This does not, however, detract from the discovery-learning approach outlined by Barbieri and Eckhardt. The goal is for students to actively analyze the language samples by completing a task (e.g., filling in a table, answering true/false questions, comparing the samples in terms of formality, etc.). Although this is not an empirical study and the effectiveness of such materials cannot be affirmed, it holds great promise for teaching reported speech with authentic language samples. More generally, the kinds of activities proposed by Barbieri and Eckhardt could be used as a model for developing grammar-focused tasks for other structures based on insights from corpora.

Although both corpus-based and literary approaches utilize authentic language samples as a source of input, a major difference is found in the type of context provided. In general, literary texts provide a lengthy context that allows the learner/reader to follow a storyline and the development of one or more characters. In sharp contrast, reading concordance lines from a corpus search provides a very different experience; learners typically see a very reduced context on either side of the key word or phrase, which can make interpretation difficult. In fact, one criticism of corpus-based pedagogy is that a corpus presents language out of its original context, which has triggered a larger debate on the authenticity of corpus examples (cf. Mishan, 2004; Widdowson, 1998, 2004). O'Keefe, McCarthy, and Carter (2007) maintain that corpus examples are authentic ("learners encounter real language as it is actually used" [p. 26]), but acknowledge that the examples are transplanted from their original context and thus are "decontextualized" in some sense. They argue for the teachers' role in careful selection of corpus examples for pedagogical purposes and in helping contextualize them for the learner.

What We Can Do . . .

1. Consider working with meaning before encouraging a focus on form.

When we find an authentic text that has many examples of a particular structure, it may be tempting to use it only as a vehicle for showing examples of the structure. In our view, this is a mistake that undermines the real value and potential of the text. Students should approach the text as a meaningful piece of language before focusing on the language therein. The rationale is that if students establish the general meaning of what is happening (e.g., what is the speaker trying to convey? what is the story about?), they are more likely to make subsequent meaning-form connections. Once they have a good sense of the context, they will be better equipped to understand grammatical choices. For example, if they understand that a character in a story is trying to influence someone else's behavior, the use of the subjunctive (or other grammatical form to realize this meaning) will make sense.

Timmis (2005) summarizes the key recommendation: "...learners will gain more from language work on a text if they have already got a general understanding of it" (p. 120). Consequently, we recommend that teachers begin with pre-reading or pre-listening tasks as they normally do to prepare their students for dealing with any text. Comprehension checks should follow, with ample time for discussion of the issues, ideas, and themes in the text. The grammar focus should take place toward the end of the pedagogical sequence via a variety of activities designed to encourage learners to notice the structure(s) in the text.

2. Work as a team to create corpus-based materials.

This is a simple, practical recommendation for teachers who want to experiment with preparing corpus-based activities for their students rather than having students interact with the corpus directly. Many studies have pointed out how time-consuming it is to work with a corpus to create DDL materials. Boulton (2010) estimated that each of the items taught in his study required half a day's work. Lin and Lee (2015) noted that teachers agreed that preparing DDL materials was time consuming, partly due to the task of choosing appropriate sentences from a long list of concordance lines. Lin and Lee give a number of practical suggestions such as reducing the number of concordance lines for each grammar concept. In addition, we recommend that teachers consider working as a team to design such materials, thus increasing their overall efficiency.

3. Use authentic texts as a springboard to target the structure you want to teach.

In all of the studies reviewed in this chapter, the authentic texts contain one or more instances of the target grammatical structure. However, this is not the only way to teach grammar in combination with authentic texts. It is possible to use an authentic text to target structures that are not necessarily represented in the text itself (this is what we are calling the 'springboard' approach). For example, a short film can be used to target past tense narration even if all the dialogue in the film is in the present tense. Teachers can set up contexts that require the students to talk about the film in the past. For example, the teacher can prepare a list of sentences in the past about the film and students work in pairs to put the events in the correct order. In other words, this approach uses the authentic text as an interesting source of content in combination with teacher-prepared sentences to target a particular grammatical concept. The role of the authentic text in this approach is slightly different, but it remains a beneficial activity since it can be set up in ways to elicit a wide range of language from the students, including advanced- and superior-level language functions (cf. Darhower, 2014 and also Myth 5).

4. Orient students to the inductive approach.

As noted earlier in this chapter, most of the research that uses authentic texts to teach grammar relies on an inductive or discovery-learning approach. Learners are guided to actively notice patterns, categorize examples, figure out rules, or speculate on reasons behind usage choices. In order for this approach to be successful, students must be willing to be active participants in the process of forming hypotheses about grammatical rules. If your students have never experienced this kind of grammar instruction, they may not react to it positively at first. In a study by Vogel, Herron, Cole, and York (2011), some participants perceived that the inductive approach could "foster more confusion, second-guessing, and frustration" (p. 368) and believed that explicit explanations would lead to more accurate output. These learners were clearly used to a deductive approach in which grammar rules were explained to them prior to engaging in output. This approach suggests that students could benefit from learner training, that is, some orientation to the inductive approach and the types of cognitive processes deemed important for learning grammar (e.g., noticing form-meaning connections). The point is that what our learners expect from grammar instruction is likely related to the kind of grammar instruction they've had in the past. As a result, we need to prepare our learners to be receptive to an inductive approach, which they may ultimately find empowering and rewarding. Of course, an inductive approach will not work with all materials. In Myth 4, we discuss how and why a teacher might opt for a deductive approach in order to focus on form during pre-listening or pre-reading.

MYTH 3

Shorter texts are more beneficial for language learners.

Every teacher has probably heard some variation of the question, "How long [does it have to be]?" in one context or another. This is a typical, almost instinctual response to writing assignments. When they are asked to read something, students will immediately look to see how many pages they need to read. In my experience (this is Eve), I've found that both students and (some) teachers are afraid of longer texts. What is the likely reaction of your students if you have them read a two-paragraph short story? And will they have the same reaction if you assign a 200-page novel? In my intermediate-level Spanish classes, students read a 125-page book in the first quarter and progress to a slightly longer (184 pages) novel in the second quarter. When I review the syllabus at the beginning of the term and explain the nature of the reading material, most students respond in the same way: They are skeptical about having to read something so long with their limited proficiency in Spanish. What they don't consider is the possibility that these longer texts might actually be easier than the shorter texts that are published in their textbook. Indeed, that is one of the issues we'd like to examine in this chapter. Our goal is to question the prevalent myth that "shorter is easier" and provide some suggestions for working with longer texts.

The qualms about longer texts apply to audiovisual material as well. I was recently asked to review some *cortometrajes* ("short films") for possible inclusion in a textbook for learners of Spanish. One film in particular was quite a bit longer than the rest (about 30 minutes). Not surprisingly, the follow-up questions for this film centered on its length and whether it could still be used effectively despite its duration. Of course, working with a 30-minute film entails certain restrictions: for example, you may not be able to do multiple viewings in class as you might do with a 10-minute film. Interestingly, I found the 30-minute film to be more accessible than some of the other films because it had relatively little dialogue, only two main characters, and natural breaks in the action where the film could be split into two or three viewing segments.

One additional anecdote to illustrate the fact that shorter is not necessarily better concerns the use of movie trailers: Charlene once observed a lesson in which the pre-service teacher had intermediate ESL students watch four short trailers. The students struggled to understand anything. The teacher's intention was not to have the students understand every word since the trailers were part of a larger lesson on movies, but the students seemed frustrated that they could not understand the videos. Although movie trailers are short, they don't work well for teaching. They are often full of cultural information presented without any plot build up to help the students understand the situation. The discourse is often choppy as the trailer jumps quickly from one scene to the next, giving students little context for the language being used. Ironically, it was likely that the students in the class could have understood a good part of the full-length movies, but they struggled to catch the colloquial language where the full context was not clear. In short, authentic material needs to be evaluated on multiple levels, with text length being only one of the factors that contribute to difficulty.

What the Research Says . . .

Intuitively, it seems that shorter texts will be easier for L2 learners since there is less information to process. This is not necessarily the case, however, since short texts may condense a lot of information. This is especially true of academic language, which is characterized by informational density, meaning that ideas are often tightly packed into a single sentence or clause. Wong Fillmore and Fillmore (2012) illustrate this with a cogent analysis of Martin Luther King's *Letter from Birmingham Jail*, which they describe as "demanding and complex, both linguistically and in its historical and philosophical content" (p. 3). Nowhere in their analysis does the length of the whole text come into play. Instead, Wong Fillmore and Fillmore point out the intricacies of focal sentences within the letter. English language learners must unpack the information in these sentences in order to ultimately gain a solid understanding of the meaning of the text. What becomes readily clear is that the complexity of the text is not a function of its overall length but rather determined by features within the text such as informational density and layered messages.

Any text—short or long—may be considered complex from a qualitative perspective. But how can we define complexity in qualitative terms? Some insights can be gleaned from the Common Core State Standards in English language arts and literacy (www.corestandards.org), which identify the following areas: (1) levels of meaning or purpose; (2) text structure; (3) language conventionality and clarity; and (4) knowledge demands placed on the reader. Again, there is no mention of text length in this conceptualization of complexity. Crucially, as noted by Bunch, Walqui, and Pearson (2014), the "difficulty [of a text] ultimately emerges from interactions among the reader, task, and available supports (p. 536). Shanahan, Fisher, and Frey (2012) give the example of Ernest Hemingway's *The Old Man and the Sea*, which would be placed at a sixth grade reading level due to its relatively simple vocabulary and short sentences, but is nevertheless more appropriate for adolescents who have a certain level of emotional maturity to understand and appreciate the themes of the novel. Young adult litera-ture is also worthy of discussion. The language is often accessible to language learners, and some novels like *The Hunger Games*, used in an example in Appendix C, contains themes that adults might find engag-ing. In sum, determining the complexity of a text based solely on its length would be misguided and further encourages the perception that shorter texts are easier for L2 learners.

One empirical study that, at first glance, seems to support the myth we are trying to dispel in this chapter is that of Leow (1997), who investigated the effects of text length on comprehension and intake of grammatical forms. (He also examined the effects of input enhance-ment—that is, bolding and underlining grammatical forms, but we won't consider that here.) Participants were second-semester learners of Spanish who read two different versions of an authentic text that gave advice for leading a healthy life. The original authentic text con-tained 631 words, whereas the shortened version was considerably reduced in length (384 words). Participants' comprehension of the text was measured with ten questions in English. The questions asked for specific information provided in the text (e.g., "The article recom-mends that you eat two things instead of bread or rolls. What are they?"). In interpreting the results of this study, it is important to keep in mind that participants had to read the passage (either the long or short version) and then answer the comprehension questions without looking back at the reading. In other words, they could not access the text while answering the comprehension questions.

The results of Leow (1997) indicate a significant main effect for text length: participants who read the shorter passage scored better on the comprehension test than those who read the longer version. Leow interprets this result as support for short texts: "These findings provide empirical evidence that supports the validity and efficacy of exposing first-year L2 learners to short authentic reading materials to facilitate reading comprehension" (p. 151). However, since learners were not allowed to access the text while answering the questions, the compre-hension test may have tapped their memory rather than their general understanding of the passage. Thus, the experimental procedure provided an inherent advantage to the group that read the shorter passage—they had less to remember. Another point worth mentioning is that the mean scores on the comprehension test were very low across the board. Even the group that read the shorter version of the text scored only 3.76 (mean) out of a maximum of 10 points. In other words, the group that had a relative advantage scored less than 50 percent on a test of comprehension. In a classroom setting, no teacher would find this to be a favorable result or take it as evidence that the students had actually understood the content.

Given these caveats, we do not believe that Leow's (1997) study should be interpreted as definitive support for the benefits of short texts, such as those included in most textbooks for L2 learners. Clearly, even short texts need to be appropriately presented if the learner is to gain adequate comprehension. Moreover, as we alluded to in Myth 1, longer texts may have benefits for language learners that shorter texts do not, especially when it comes to thematic continuity and repetition of vocabulary. As suggested by Allen, Bernhardt, Berry, and Demel (1988), "lengthier texts may be more cohesive and, hence, more interesting for learners (p. 170). In what follows, we examine the ways in which lengthier texts may provide favorable conditions for language acquisition.

Vocabulary Repetition within Longer Texts

One of the primary ways in which longer texts can promote language acquisition, and vocabulary gains in particular, is through the repetition of lexical items. Learning a new word is crucially dependent on the number of encounters or exposures to that particular word. In general, the probability of learning a new word from context with a single exposure is low, but with multiple exposures (generally between 8 and 10), the learner has a reasonably good chance of learning a particular word (cf. Schmitt, 2008, Webb, 2014). The idea is that L2 learners can pick up vocabulary (also known as *incidental* learning) from reading if the text provides enough opportunities to encounter the same words repeatedly. Longer texts, such as complete novels, are good candidates for meeting this basic condition of vocabulary recycling.

Pellicer-Sánchez and Schmitt (2010) conducted a study to determine how well certain words could be learned incidentally by reading an unmodified authentic novel (Achebe's *Things Fall Apart*). The participants were advanced learners of English who read the novel for pleasure, without any indication that vocabulary would later be tested. The results were favorable in terms of demonstrating a good rate of incidental learning: Participants were able to recognize the meaning of 43 percent of the target words. In line with their predictions, the authors found a much higher rate of learning for words that were frequently repeated (10–17 times) in the text: Participants were able to recognize the meaning of 84 percent of these words. Despite these favorable results, Pellicer-Sánchez and Schmitt remind us that it is difficult to attain complete mastery of a new word from incidental exposure alone. Nevertheless, we want to emphasize that their study is a prime example of the fact that longer texts (e.g., a novel of 67,000 words) provide repeated exposures to vocabulary in another language.

Another study that documents the facilitative effect of vocabulary repetition in authentic texts is Kweon and Kim (2008). Their participants, native speakers of Korean enrolled in a university-level reading course, read three chapter books that totaled roughly 134,000 words or 640 pages of text. The researchers examined frequent content words that were repeated within the texts, sorting them into different categories based on the number of repetitions. For example, words like *warden* (136 tokens), *canteen* (52 tokens), and *squid* (46 tokens) were among the most frequent content words in these books. Kweon and Kim tested how well 367 words from the texts were learned incidentally, relying primarily on a self-report measure (i.e., participants indicated how well they knew each word on a three-point scale). Although self-reports can overestimate what learners actually know, the results are nevertheless promising. Participants' mean scores increased significantly from the pre-test to the post-test, with gains as high as 40 percent. Not surprisingly, words that were more frequent (i.e., recycled more often) were learned better and were less susceptible to attrition.

Furthermore, Kweon and Kim point out that some low-frequency words, which were "salient and significant" to the storyline (p. 208), were also learned and retained. The authors argue for "using authentic texts *of substantial length*" (p. 195, emphasis added) to better understand the nature of incidental vocabulary acquisition from reading.

With shorter texts, it is more difficult to get this degree of vocabulary recycling. To achieve this aim with shorter texts, you need to read several texts on the same topic (also known as *narrow reading*, as discussed briefly in Myth 1). Gardner (2008) analyzed how vocabulary is repeated in a large corpus of authentic texts for children (fifth grade level), distinguishing between narrative and expository texts. He focused only on words beyond the 1,000 most frequent words in English (the top 1,000 words are repeated so frequently in all kinds of texts that we don't need to worry about them). Gardner's analysis showed that the greatest amount of vocabulary recycling occurs in expository texts that have a tight theme. For example, the analysis of four texts on the topic of mummies revealed that 97 words were repeated six times or more (e.g., *tombs, pyramid, buried, preserved, Egypt*). This figure comes from a total of 20,000 running words, or approximately 80 pages of text. Note that the purpose of Gardner's study was to compare vocabulary across texts and not within a single text, like in the study by Pellicer-Sánchez and Schmitt (2010).

The pedagogical takeaway from Gardner's (2008) study is clear: If learners read several texts on the same topic, especially around a tightly connected theme, they will gain the benefit of numerous exposures to specific vocabulary words. And there is good reason to believe that this kind of recycling translates into actual vocabulary learning. Kang (2015) conducted a study with two groups of Korean high school students. Both groups read a main text on secondhand smoke. The narrow reading group read three additional texts on the topic of secondhand smoke whereas the comparison group read three unrelated texts. Afterward, both groups were tested on 15 target words that appeared in the main text related to secondhand smoke (e.g., *evidence, ban, asthma, eliminate*). Kang's results show that the narrow reading group performed significantly better than the comparison group on tests of receptive and productive vocabulary knowledge. On the exit questionnaire, one student from the narrow reading group reflected on his learning in this way:

> Because many words are related to each other in terms of meaning and belong to the theme of secondhand smoking, it helped me learn the words. In the texts, words "asthma" and "respiratory diseases" constantly occurred together in the texts. (Kang, 2015, 176).

Finally, it is important to keep in mind Kang's study tested narrow reading with relatively short texts (450 words each). But there are obvious parallels between narrow reading and reading a single, longer text. In fact, Schmitt and Carter (2000) suggest that "following a storyline within a single book should yield much the same facilitation as reading several separate articles on the same news story" (p. 8).

Following a storyline is ultimately what keeps us turning the pages of a good novel or draws us into watching a television series. But are there any language learning gains to be made from watching episodes of a television series? Rodgers and Webb (2011) provide evidence to suggest that watching successive episodes of one program is a potentially good way of learning L2 vocabulary. They analyzed a corpus of 1.3 million words comprised of transcripts from popular TV dramas such as *House, Grey's Anatomy, CSI,* and *Alias.* Their goal was to compare the vocabulary in a related series (e.g., successive episodes of *House*) versus the vocabulary in unrelated episodes from several different television dramas. Their results reveal exactly the kind of vocabulary recycling that should favor incidental learning: Related TV episodes contained fewer word families overall and more repetition of low-frequency words (in their study, low-frequency included words beyond the most common 4,000 words). For example, of the nearly 6,000 low-frequency running words in *House,* approximately 2,500 were from word families that were encountered 10 or more times. Rodgers and Webb advocate using episodes of a TV series in the same way as an extensive reading program in order to provide learners with copious amounts of authentic, aural input. Finally, it is worth noting that an entire season of a TV show can be considered, from our vantage point, a single lengthy text that has been spliced into episodes by the producers for the purposes of advertising and distribution.

This section has emphasized vocabulary recycling as a key element of longer texts. Vocabulary recycling is closely related to another beneficial characteristic, which some have labeled thematic continuity (cf. Maxim, 2002). *Thematic continuity* means that there is an opportunity for background knowledge to build cumulatively as the text unfolds. For example, a television series has reoccurring characters and themes, which allows the viewer to gradually become familiar with the setting, the relationships among the characters, and the main plot. Rodgers (2013) demonstrated this in a large-scale study with Japanese EFL learners who viewed full-length episodes of an American TV drama. Participants watched ten successive episodes of *Chuck* over the course of a semester, for a total viewing time of approximately seven hours (each episode lasted an average of 42 minutes). Rodgers documented significant comprehension gains from the first to the tenth episode, which he attributed to the gradual accumulation of background information. Rodgers proposes that, as learners continue viewing, the previous episodes function as advance organizers. In this way, thematic continuity reduces the burden on learners, allowing them to comprehend more as they build knowledge of the text.

Yang (2001) also appeals to thematic continuity in explaining his choice of two Agatha Christie mystery novels for his ESL learners. Since the same characters appear in both books, students "free themselves from the need to struggle through background knowledge each time they pick up a new piece" (Yang, 2001, p. 454). Based on interviews with some of his participants, Yang explains that the students initially found the reading difficult because of the intimidation factor (most of them had not read a full-length English novel before). Yet, the interviews and questionnaire data confirm that reading became progressively easier after they had finished several chapters and all of the major characters had been introduced. Yang's data suggest that thematic continuity, which is especially important in unfolding stories such as mysteries, allowed the students to understand the plot in an authentic text and thus motivated them to continue reading.

Shorter texts are unlikely to provide the same facilitative effects in terms of thematic continuity and vocabulary repetition. Nevertheless, shorter texts are routinely used with other pedagogical objectives. In the next section, we address the specific uses of film clips (e.g., individual scenes from a film or television episode), which have gained popularity in many L2 contexts. This approach represents *intensive viewing*, meaning that short clips serve to teach some specific aspect of language or culture.

Intensive Viewing with Short Film Clips

Language learning is constrained by the classroom seat time, especially in foreign language contexts. The reality is such that teachers may have only three to five hours per week in the classroom with the students. This situation naturally disfavors the use of longer texts such complete novels and feature films. Conversely, it favors the use of short films, which have an average running time of 15 minutes (cf., Sundquist, 2010), and film clips that are only several minutes in length. In this section, we examine the research that addresses particular uses of film clips for language learning purposes, highlighting both advantages and disadvantages.

Kaiser (2011) describes a project at the Berkeley Language Center that resulted in an online, searchable database of foreign language film clips (http://blcvideoclips.berkeley.edu). Each clip is maximally four minutes long and is tagged for its linguistic, cultural, and pragmatic/functional content. For example, instructors can search for film clips in the target language that show greetings, telephone conversations, or narrations. Kaiser describes the various pedagogical applications of these film clips such as improving listening comprehension, examining language choices (e.g., the meaning of particular words in context), and developing students' cultural awareness. Kaiser argues that viewing a film clip is akin to doing a "close reading" of a scene (p. 234). In comparison to viewing an entire film, Kaiser maintains that film clips have the following advantages: they can be replayed multiple times in class; the quantity of the language is manageable; they offer the instructor more options in terms of assignments; and they allow in-depth analysis of one scene. Moreover, film clips can be a valuable resource for the teacher who wishes to incorporate authentic cultural material that expands on the textbook's themes. For example, when working with a chapter on family and wedding vocabulary (e.g., *to marry, bride, groom*), film clips tagged for *wedding* could be used not only to contextualize the vocabulary but also to expand on cultural issues surrounding wedding traditions or attitudes toward marriage.

Kaiser (2011) also mentions some potential pitfalls of working with film clips. In our view, the most important one is the risk of decontextualization: "Isolating a specific scene from a film decontextualizes it and some interpretive meaning is lost. Scenes in a film are often in dialogue with one another . . ." (p. 234). Viewing one scene from a film allows for in-depth analysis of that scene, and especially the language used, but it does not permit the gradual building of background knowledge that we described earlier using the term *thematic continuity*. As a result, teachers will have to work hard to contextualize a film clip so that students can engage in the type of interpretation activities that Kaiser advocates. As a case in point, the scenes described by Kaiser in the article (e.g., scenes from the film *Moscow Doesn't Believe in Tears*) require extensive explanation so that the reader—without having seen the entire film—can appreciate what kinds of analysis can be done with the clip. To overcome the lack of background knowledge, Tognozzi (2010) recommends that teachers choose film clips with dialogue that is "self-contained," which allows students to "understand the conversation without knowing what happened earlier" (p. 74). Tognozzi also provides examples of interesting activities that can be done with film clips to promote oral fluency, listening comprehension, and cultural knowledge. For example, students (intermediate and advanced learners of Italian) were asked to research a cultural topic depicted in the film clips they watched.

The use of short film clips or individual scenes from television shows (e.g., sitcoms, soap operas) is an important component of pragmatics instruction. Researchers have lamented that textbook dialogues often provide a distorted or impoverished model of various speech acts (Boxer & Pickering, 1995; Eisenchlas, 2011, Grant & Starks, 2001, among others), and consequently, many have advocated for the use of film/TV to provide more realistic models of native speaker interactions (cf. Martínez-Flor, 2008; Rose, 2001; Washburn, 2001). In this line of research, film clips or short scenes from TV shows are used to promote pragmatic awareness, either through deductive or inductive teaching methods. For example, Washburn describes her approach to using sitcoms as "realistic and stimulating examples" (p. 26), having learners identify speech acts and violations of pragmatic norms. The sample lesson in Washburn is built around short video clips, generally 10–30 seconds in length, which are replayed numerous times during the course of the lesson. Similarly, Fernández-Guerra and Martínez-Flor (2003) provide concrete examples of how to use scenes from films—as short as one minute each—for the purposes of illustrating different speech acts (e.g., requests).

A short film clip illustrates a speech act; learners don't need to watch an entire feature film to observe a compliment and response or a greeting and leave-taking. Indeed, the strategy of viewing several short clips that illustrate the same speech act seems to be particularly useful for pragmatics instruction. Finally, it is worth mentioning that using short film clips, which allows for intensive work with one scene, is not mutually exclusive with watching the entire film or episode. For example, Washburn (2001) describes a number of extension activities that students can do outside of class, including ongoing viewing of episodes of a particular sitcom. Even if time constraints prevent students from watching a feature film or a complete episode of a sitcom during class, this is a rather weak argument for avoiding longer texts altogether. Instead, teachers should find viable ways of incorporating longer texts for viewing/reading into the course structure and also provide pedagogical support to keep students on track (see the **What We Can Do** section).

Comparison of Short versus Long Texts

In our experience, longer texts are generally perceived as too difficult on two levels—too difficult for the learner and too difficult for the teacher to implement in class given the time constraints of most language learning contexts. Nevertheless, we want to emphasize that longer texts may actually require less effort in terms of activating and/or providing background knowledge. Consider the fact that if you ask learners to read three short stories on unrelated topics, you will need to activate or build relevant background knowledge for each story. In contrast, if you ask learners to read a longer narrative, you will need to do similar work at the pre-reading stage, but only once. Instead, with a longer text, the teacher's efforts will shift to making sure learners understand the development of the storyline.

In arguing for the merits of longer texts, we are not recommending that teachers abandon the use of short texts. As mentioned in the discussion of film clips, shorter texts have distinct pedagogical advantages and have been shown to be effective in supplementing textbook presentation of culture and pragmatics. Short texts can be re-played, re-read, and re-analyzed on multiple levels during class time. These tangible benefits come at a price: the teacher will need to contextualize the text in order for learners to understand who the characters are, what their relationship is, the cultural references in the text, etc. This contextualization is especially important for short texts that are isolated from a larger whole (e.g., a film clip or a fragment of a book).

Since vocabulary research has figured prominently in this chapter, we note that short texts may be conducive to *intentional* vocabulary learning, meaning that explicit attention is drawn to particular lexical items and students do a variety of activities to consolidate their knowledge of the target words. For example, in reading a short story, five words that are significant to the plot can be targeted. Explicit attention is devoted to these five words in class and later students can do some exercises (e.g., matching words and their definitions, writing original sentences with the words) to strengthen their knowledge of these items. Schmitt (2008) and other researchers argue that intentional learning should be a major component of L2 vocabulary instruction, in conjunction with opportunities for *incidental* vocabulary learning. Schmitt explains that "intentional and incidental approaches are not only complementary, but positively require each other" (p. 353). Similarly, longer texts provide crucial opportunities for encountering words in context multiple times (thus favoring incidental learning), whereas shorter texts allow the teacher to devote explicit attention to a small number of words (thus favoring intentional learning).

Finally, it is worth mentioning that text length is obviously a continuous variable and also a relative concept. For example, a 15-minute short film will be relatively long for a group of beginning-level learners who have only been exposed to short fragments of audiovisual material in the L2. A 1,500-word short story is not as long as a complete novel, and yet it is longer than the short stories typically included in textbooks. Table 3.1 summarizes the main differences between short(er) and long(er) texts that we have highlighted in this chapter.

Although time constraints can make it difficult to work with longer texts in class, this does not mean that longer texts should be taken completely out of the classroom setting. Webb (2015) explains the importance of having a classroom component to an extensive viewing program. Although eventually we want students to engage in regular, uninterrupted viewing of television in the L2 outside of class, Webb explains that "if extensive viewing is dismissed as belonging solely out-

Table 3.1: Comparison of Short and Long Texts

Short(er) Texts	Long(er) Texts
Can be presented multiple times in a class session (repeated viewing, listening, reading).	Time constraints make it more difficult to work with in class; may be assigned for reading or viewing outside of class.
Teacher will need to activate background knowledge for each text separately.	Thematic continuity; background knowledge builds on itself.
Little or no vocabulary recycling; new words will need explicit attention (intentional learning).	Vocabulary recycling facilitative of incidental learning.

side of the classroom, then many students may not take the task of viewing seriously or quickly give up" (p. 166). In the classroom, teachers can support the comprehension process with pre-viewing and post-viewing activities and as well encouraging students who may have achieved only partial comprehension.

What We Can Do . . .

1. Break longer texts into manageable pieces.

This simple piece of advice applies equally to written or audiovisual texts. For example, Abrams (2014) had her students watch a feature film in 10- to 15-minute segments once a week for seven weeks. Maxim (2002) had his students read a complete romance novel in 20-minute segments during class. The same recommendation is also important for out-of-class reading/viewing, since L2 learners tend to feel overwhelmed or intimidated by longer texts. With intermediate learners, I have found that assigning shorter segments of a novel (10–15 pages) works much better than assigning a longer segment (30 pages) because teachers can monitor students' comprehension at regular intervals and guide students who may have gained only partial understanding. With longer segments, it is more likely that you will "lose" students who are not understanding what they are reading.

2. Experiment with audio-assisted reading.

With longer written texts, L2 learners have more difficulty staying on task; they may get discouraged quickly (and thus give up) or get distracted by looking up too many words in the dictionary. One type of pedagogical support that can help learners stay on track when reading longer texts is a simultaneous audio rendition of the text. This is known as **audio-assisted reading** or **reading while listening**. There is now a growing body of L2 research that shows the benefits of reading while listening, such as improved reading rates and comprehension (Chang & Millett, 2015), increased interest and concentration (Chang, 2009), and greater vocabulary learning (Brown, Waring, & Donkaewbua, 2008; Webb & Chang, 2015). For example, students in Chang and Millett's study reported that the dramatic narration and sound effects of the audiobook made the stories more interesting. Although this research was done in the context of graded readers, we see no reason why the benefits would not extend to authentic texts (audio-assisted reading is not new to L1 literacy research, a context in which authentic texts are used. See Larson, 2015, for a recent example). Advancements in technology have made audiobooks easily accessible on various electronic readers (e.g., Kindles, iPads) and for a wide range of authentic texts.

3. Remind students that reading/viewing will get easier as they progress.

From a learner's perspective, there is often a psychological barrier or sense of intimidation when confronted with longer texts intended for native speakers. In order to create a supportive environment for reading/viewing longer texts, it is important to remind learners that precise comprehension is not a requirement (cf. Webb, 2015). Moreover, students must be reminded that things will get easier. We echo the advice of Rodgers and Webb (2011) who suggest that "the learners should be warned that they may not understand everything at first, but that comprehension will improve [in successive episodes]" (p. 712). Comprehension improves because vocabulary that was initially unfamiliar has been repeated enough times to become (at least partially) known and the characters have become familiar enough for the viewer to anticipate their behavior. As we've shown in this chapter, longer authentic texts—both audiovisual and written—can create a snowball effect due to vocabulary recycling and thematic continuity. It certainly cannot hurt to inform students of these benefits.

MYTH 4

Activating background knowledge or making a word list is sufficient to prepare students for authentic texts.

In the Real World . . .

I once observed a skilled pre-service teacher in an advanced ESL class doing a lesson on the topic of affirmative action. (This is Charlene.) She had chosen interesting materials that were at the appropriate level for the students. The reading included some historical information on the civil rights movement as well as some information related to race and diversity. As a pre-reading activity, the teacher showed a picture of Martin Luther King, Jr., and asked the students who was in the picture and why he was famous. They already knew who Martin Luther King, Jr., was and why he was famous, but they knew nothing about affirmative action and thus struggled to understand the passage. What the teacher had done was activate the students' existing knowledge, which was a good step, but she had not taught them any new information that they needed to know to understand the passage.

After this incident, I realized that many language textbooks fall short of actually teaching students important information to help them understand listening and reading materials; they often include only a picture or a question, such as *What do you know about X?* This teacher was likely drawing on pre-reading activities that she had seen in textbooks. We can call such a step *schema activation* to distinguish it from *schema building*. I also realized that I had not done a good job of helping my pre-service teachers understand what was needed to help students with current, culturally relevant material. To illustrate this point with my pre-service teachers, I gave them a current news story from an English language Taiwanese newspaper. The article discussed a recent political debate going on in Taiwan. As a pre-reading activity, I asked the students some questions such as *Where is Taiwan?* and *What do you know about Taiwan?* It demonstrated that even though the students knew something about Taiwan, they could not understand a news story in English because they did not have the appropriate background knowledge. I used this example to show the difference between schema activation (tapping into what they already knew) and schema building (teaching them new information), and to emphasize that schema activation was not sufficient to help them understand the passage even though they were very advanced or native speakers of English.

What the Research Says . . .

In this chapter, we will discuss what the research says about how to help students understand authentic reading or listening materials before they read or listen to the materials. We argue that teachers need to go beyond what many textbooks do, which is to ask questions about or show them pictures of what students already know and to give them lists of vocabulary. We address research on three topics: topic and cultural familiarity, formal schema knowledge (i.e., the organization of the text), and the vocabulary and grammar of authentic materials.

Topic and Cultural Familiarity

Much early research suggested that students understand a text better if they are familiar with the content, and in fact, one study directly tested the effects of topic familiarity on reading comprehension using authentic materials. Brantmeier (2003) conducted a study with students of Spanish by giving them shortened authentic short stories with glosses added. One story was expected to appeal more to men (a passage about boxing) and one to women (a passage about a wife). Although Brantmeier found that the men understood the boxing passage better and the women the wife passage, significant topic effects were found only with the wife passage. It's not clear why only one passage showed a topic familiarity effect, but it could have been that one passage was inherently easier than the other; conducting research with authentic materials is difficult because the researcher cannot control all the variables related to text comprehension. This study suggests that an unfamiliar topic will make a passage more difficult to understand, but only if the language is challenging. Put another way, topic familiarity can have a facilitative effect on the comprehension of difficult language, and therefore making sure the students have some familiarity before they read is important.

Related research has looked at cultural schema, which is somewhat similar to topic familiarity or content schema. Erten and Razi (2009) explained that cultural schema is abstract but can help readers or listeners by decreasing the cognitive load if the information in the text meets their expectations. They used an example from Alptekin (2008) that illustrates how even a description of a breakfast scene might affect British versus Turkish readers differently because those two groups tend to have different expectations about what is eaten for breakfast. In their study, Erten and Razi used a story written in English about New York City. One group received a version of the story that had been changed to take place in a Turkish city with the names of Turkish streets and landmarks and to include Turkish characters. They called the revised passage the *nativized* version. Using a written recall to test comprehension, the researchers found that students reading the nativized version were able to recall significantly more of the story. This suggests that it is important for teachers to provide students with the cultural information that they need before reading the text. Furthermore, Erten and Razi included not only two groups who read different story versions but also two additional groups who read the two versions with a pre-reading activity and several while-reading activities. They found that the activities did not help the students reading the unmodified version of the story, only the nativized version. Crucially, the pre-reading activity in their study simply asked students to predict the storyline; the activity did not appear to provide the students with cultural knowledge. This emphasizes the fact that simply asking students to reflect on what they already know may not be enough to help them understand unfamiliar material. One benefit of authentic materials is exposure to the target culture, but instructors will have to ensure that they devote a fair amount of time to providing students with the cultural knowledge that they do not have.

In addition to showing the effects of topic familiarity on learners' comprehension of the materials, other research has studied its effects on their learning of vocabulary and grammar. In other words, teaching students the background knowledge that they need to understand the text may also help them learn vocabulary and grammar incidentally. Studies have investigated the role of topic familiarity, demonstrating positive effects for lexical inferencing (Pulido, 2007) and form recognition for the Spanish future tense (Leeser, 2007).

Considering all of these studies together, we can assume that background knowledge affects text comprehension and some aspects of learning while reading. The study by Erten and Razi (2009) yielded important findings, but note that they did not attempt to teach background knowledge. In contrast, Chang and Read (2006) conducted an experimental study of different types of pre-listening activities, one of which was designed to provide students with background information (i.e., schema building not schema activation) before listening to a text. They also included a group who previewed the comprehension questions, a group who heard the material three times, and a vocabulary instruction group. They found that background knowledge helped both the low- and high-proficiency EFL learners but that listening multiple times helped only the high-proficiency learners. Although the previewing of questions was also helpful, the vocabulary instruction had no effect—a point to which we will return later. Finally, although Chang and Read opted for a non-authentic text in their experiment, we believe the results are clearly applicable to authentic texts as well.

Formal Schema

Finally, in addition to background knowledge, knowledge of the structure of a text can help students understand authentic materials. This knowledge is called **formal schema** or **discourse structure knowledge**. Early related research by Carrell (1984) showed ESL students could recall a passage better if it followed a clearer organizational pattern such as cause-effect or problem-solution as opposed to texts that were a collection of descriptions. She followed up this study (Carrell, 1987) by comparing the effects of content familiarity and rhetorical structure familiarity. As expected, both the familiar content and structure aided recall, although content familiarity had a greater effect. In both of these studies, the more difficult rhetorical structures were not intentionally manipulated to be specific to one culture but rather simply less clearly organized. The point is that rhetorical structure can affect comprehension (as measured by recall of a passage). Thus, second language learners facing new genres found in authentic materials may struggle if either the organization is not transparent or if it differs from the organization of a genre in their native language.

Chu, Swaffar, and Charney (2002) looked more specifically at cultural differences in text organization for Taiwanese students learning English. In their study, they used authentic editorials in English from a bilingual Taiwanese publication. These editorials followed what has been called a *qi-cheng-zhuang-he* style that differs from Western expository style. The authors used these English texts written for a Taiwanese publication and modified them in a variety of ways, including putting background information and a thesis statement at the beginning of the editorials. They found that the Taiwanese students could recall more of the passages written in the *qi-cheng-zhuang-he* structure. This study should be interpreted somewhat cautiously because the authors did not provide the passages so it's not clear what the modification to the so-called English style looked like; however, the research does point to the fact that a familiar organization can facilitate comprehension and recall.

Regardless of whether the authentic materials match the structure of the genre in the students' native language, constructing pre-reading or pre-listening activities that focus on text organization can be helpful. Although we do not know of any intervention studies (i.e., experimental studies that test some type of instruction) that teach culturally specific rhetorical organization to help second language learners, Jiang (2012) conducted a longitudinal experimental study over 16 weeks with Chinese students studying English. One group received instruction using graphic organizers to help them understand the structures of the texts that they read while the other did not. The group that regularly used the graphic organizers performed better on a test of discourse organization and on a test of reading comprehension. The results on the reading comprehension test did not, however, persist on a delayed post-test seven weeks after instruction. Although this study cannot confirm the lasting effects of the awareness of text structure, there is certainly evidence that knowledge of text structure can improve reading comprehension, which should make learners feel more confident when approaching authentic texts.

Dealing with Difficult Language

With regard to vocabulary, we suspect that many teachers pre-teach vocabulary related to specific reading or listening materials and certainly, so do many textbooks. Sometimes word lists with their translations or definitions are provided. With regard to listening, the Chang and Read (2006) study discussed earlier suggests that pre-teaching words might not be helpful as a pre-listening activity because students do not have time to access the new word knowledge and because listening for words can direct their attention away from other aspects of a passage, a point confirmed in the student interviews from the Chang and Read study.

For reading, glosses will help learners understand more, but there are some problems with relying on word lists and glosses. First, vocabulary research overwhelmingly suggests that involvement or engagement with words helps retention (see the summary by Laufer & Hulstijn, 2001); simply providing definitions does not encourage students to search for the meaning of the word or evaluate if they are using it correctly, two factors that help retention. Activities such as filling in the blank or using the words in meaningful contexts better promote retention. Also, word lists with definitions do not show the word in context. In a study comparing materials from different academic fields, Hyland and Tse (2007) examined how certain frequent words from the Academic Word List (Coxhead, 2000) are used across fields, noting that certain common words, such as *process*, are used quite differently. They conclude that "by breaking into single words items which may be better learnt as wholes, vocabulary lists simultaneously misrepresent discipline-specific meanings and mislead students" (p. 246). The point of their study is to argue against the use of generic academic word lists, but we feel that the study highlights the importance of presenting words in context, especially for more advanced learners. Although word lists may be a useful first step in vocabulary learning (Folse, 2004), examining words in context allows students to learn collocations (which words generally appear before or after the target word) and other aspects of usage.

Although vocabulary instruction is important in helping students understand authentic texts, students may also benefit from a focus on difficult grammar that might appear in the texts. In Myth 2, we talked about using a text in an inductive approach to grammar instruction, namely, students read for meaning and try to infer how a particular structure is used. Here, we want to suggest that a different approach be used to focus on particular sentences that may frustrate students as they are encountered. This can be a problem particularly when students are listening; they can get stuck on a sentence and lose track of what they are listening to. However, we know of no studies that specifically examine the pre-teaching of difficult sentences or grammar in general on text comprehension. Instead, we turn to research by Schleppegrell, Achugar, and Oteíza (2004), who emphasize the importance of focusing on structures that are related to the genre and topic students are reading.

Schleppegrell et al. (2004) argued for a focus on linguistic analysis to help students understand history texts in a content-based instruction context. In their article, they included examples of structures used in history texts that may cause students to misunderstand history textbooks. They argued that teachers need to be able to explain, through a functional analysis of language, how historians construct meaning. We note that they use a systemic functional approach to describing language, which we will not elaborate on here, but we echo their call for teachers to focus on how grammar is used to express meaning in authentic texts. The grammar points that teachers choose to focus on, of course, depend on the language and material, but we include one example from Schleppegrell et al. One feature of academic writing is nominalization, a feature often discussed in the systemic functional approach to linguistics. The second sentence in the extract has two nominalizations that a reader will have to interpret by referring back to the information in the previous sentence.

> In 1819, 11 states in the Union permitted slavery and 11 did not. The Senate—with two members from each state—was therefore evenly balanced between slave and free states. The admission of a new state would upset that balance. (p. 79)

Schleppegrell et al. focus on the difficulties in the texts but do not go into detail on how to teach the difficult structures or when to teach them except to say that students can be guided as they read to answer questions for which they will need to understand certain grammatical and functional relationships. We believe that once students have some background knowledge related to the topic, Schleppegrell et al.'s approach can be used by teachers to focus on such difficult sentences *before* they read. The students can be given sentences from the reading with the difficult grammar features underlined (see previous extract). This close reading of the underlined items will raise their awareness of the structure and ensure they understand the sentences before reading the texts. An added possible benefit is that the sentences will alert the students to some of the specific details of the content, as opposed to main ideas, that they will encounter when they read.

Many studies describe how certain grammatical structures might be used in a subset of authentic texts. For example, Millar, Budgell, and Fuller (2013) examined medical journals and provided a quantitative description of how the passive voice was used in the articles. They described which section of the articles it was used in (the passive was used mostly in the methods and results sections) as well as which verbs were more likely to be used in the passive compared to the active (for example, the verb *associate* was more likely to be used in the passive than the active). Many assume that these types of descriptions will help teachers create grammar-in-context materials that will help their learners read authentic materials. Unfortunately, the studies do not examine grammar previewing as a pre-reading activity; instead, they focus on the grammar of authentic materials as a way to help students write, such as Bloch (2009), which is discussed in Myth 5.

Nevertheless, it seems that in a language-for-specific-purpose (LSP) class, it would make sense to exploit the corpus-based research that includes grammatical descriptions of specialized texts. These studies can be used to help teachers decide which structures are associated with the texts and examples can be extracted before the students read.

This chapter has emphasized that getting students to draw on their background knowledge can be helpful, but it is not always sufficient to prepare students for authentic texts. There is plenty of research showing that familiarity with the content and organization of the text can be important in understanding the text and in helping students learn language from the texts. Overall, the research suggests there is value in teaching students about content and the text formats that they might not be familiar with and helping them with challenging sentence structures before they read.

What We Can Do . . .

1. Provide the students with background knowledge.

Students can and should be given authentic material that includes unfamiliar content so that they learn more about the target cultures related to the target language. For beginners, teachers can give students a list of events, people, or places that are important in the reading or listening materials. For homework, they can read about the items in their native language on, for example, Wikipedia. Students can then be asked to write one sentence about each item in the target language. For beginners, asking them to read authentic materials as a pre-reading task to other authentic materials can be too challenging, so having them read in their native language outside of class is likely more effective. For students at the intermediate level, teachers can prepare a mini-lecture on the topic of the material using simple language with visual support. Students can be given graphic organizers to fill out while they listen to the teacher's lecture. In this activity, the students will first hear non-authentic language with the goal of learning the content.

2. Teach proper nouns and use maps and pictures to provide cultural information.

As previously discussed, cultural information that may not even be central to the authentic text may make material harder to understand simply because unknown names and places may increase the cognitive load. The problem is magnified while listening because students might not be aware that what they heard was a proper noun and may get stuck trying to figure out the meaning of the unknown word. There are a few possible ways that teachers can prepare students. As with teaching background knowledge, teachers can give students lists of names or places for them to review before class or at home. If the students will be listening to authentic material, the teacher can do a short dictation containing the various names so that students can hear them. If the cultural information is geographic, the instructor can do a listening activity with a map that helps students orient to the location of the places mentioned. Certainly, pictures will be helpful, too: Teachers can give students pictures of locations that they have to discuss in groups or write about before listening or reading.

Sometimes the cultural knowledge will be more complex and will require more extensive instruction. For example, the students might listen to a news story about a holiday or read a short story about a relationship between two people that might differ in significant ways from their own experience. In these cases, the instructor can treat the material as new content and teach the student the new information. Another option is to ask students to answer questions that will direct their attention to the unfamiliar information. After a class discussion of the questions, the students can listen to or read the material a second time.

3. Teach discourse organization.

Whether the structure of the authentic text is new to the students or simply not transparent, understanding what to expect will help the students understand the material. One way to prepare students is to give them graphic organizers and predict what they will hear or read in each section. If the students are reading something with headings, those can be used in the organizer. For shorter readings without headings or for listening material, the students can be given an outline with the first sentence of each paragraph or logical sections. This outline not only helps students understand the organization of the passage but also forces them to carefully read some of the sentences ahead of time. After the students predict the information, they can listen or read to see if they were correct. Even if the students cannot predict the content because it is too unfamiliar, such an activity will increase their awareness of the structure of the text. A focus on the structure of a text can also be done as a post-reading or listening activity to help prepare students for other texts of the same genre. For stories, instructors will have to be more creative, but they may be able to draw a flow chart with hints to key events.

Some texts, such as lectures, lend themselves to a discussion of metadiscourse language such as *in the next section, to conclude, going back to my last point,* and so on. Drawing learners' attention to these phrases, such as underlining them before reading, will give the learners clues to the organization of the material.

4. Teach vocabulary in context in ways that will promote retention.

Laufer and Hulstijn (2001), as previously mentioned, were able to isolate factors from a large number of studies that led to students' retention of words. They found that searching for the meaning of the word, needing to use it, and evaluating if it is used correctly will lead to retention. Pre-reading activities that meet these criteria and show the word used in context can be created. The easiest type of exercise to create is to take sentences from the listening or reading material and create a fill-in-the-blank activity with a word bank for which students need to look up the definition of the words. In this way, the students have to manipulate the words and evaluate whether or not the words fit into the sentence. In addition, the students are seeing the words in context before reading the material. In a listening activity, the students will have first read several sentences, which should allow them to focus on larger chunks of texts as opposed to single words. Another option might be to take out-of-order sentences from text with new words underlined and ask students to put the sentences in order. For yet another variation, see Appendix D.

A dictogloss (also called *dictocomp)* is another activity that encourages students to use new vocabulary (see Appendix E). For beginners, this activity is often best done after reading or listening to new material, but for more advanced students, the first paragraph of a reading or first part of a lecture can be used in a dictogloss as a preliminary activity to teach new vocabulary. To do this, the teacher can give students a list of new words and go over the meaning. Then, the students listen to a passage a few times after which they must reconstruct the passage using the new words. This activity will not only get the students to use the new words but will also serve as a preview of the beginning of the material for them.

5. Focus on difficult sentence structures before students read or listen.

A simple way to focus on specific sentences is to do a dictation activity with the difficult sentences or with sentences that contain the focal grammar point. The students may struggle, but then the teacher can show the sentences and talk about the structures in question. Another option, for more advanced students, is to give the students the sentences and ask them to try to paraphrase the sentence or connected sentences. Some grammatical structures may also lend themselves to fill-in-the-blank activities. For example, sentences with difficult verb forms can be given with the verbs deleted for students to fill in. These activities can be done not only as pre-listening and pre-reading activities but also in between repeated listenings or readings of the material.

Authentic texts can be used to teach only listening and reading.

When I was getting my MA TESOL degree, I understood the importance of using authentic materials to teach reading, but I did not think much about using them to teach writing. (This is Charlene.) Upon finishing my degree, I taught a low-level community college ESL writing class. The textbook that I was given included units that began with model essays. The book, like many textbooks of that era, was organized according to rhetorical structures such as narrative, compare-contrast, and cause-effect. I noticed immediately that each essay had a clear organization and that the vocabulary was simple and had been purposely limited. In addition, the model essays were incredibly boring. From a teaching reading perspective, I knew that the sample essays were problematic because they did not resemble anything that the students might read in their other classes. For some reason, however, I did not realize that such essays might actually be counterproductive to teaching writing, a productive skill. Indeed, when I collected my students' first assignment, I saw that each body paragraph began with an ordinal number while the last paragraphs all ended with *in conclusion*. I realized the problem, but I did not know how to fix it, nor did I know how to create a writing curriculum that would move the students beyond what I later learned was called *a five-paragraph essay*. It did not occur to me that I should have used some authentic materials to help students write more interesting and meaningful pieces with more sophisticated language.

A year later, I was asked to teach a class for international teaching assistants who had to improve their English speaking skills so that they could teach at a university. I noticed that some of the students' voices were monotone; they did not use stress to emphasize points, highlight new vocabulary, or focus on important concepts. Such a style of speaking can be particularly problematic when teaching, as my students would soon be doing. During that time, I happened to enjoy listening to a local newscaster who provided short eloquent editorials. As I was listening to him, I realized that he was skilled at using stress to make his point. I recorded and transcribed a few two-minute editorials. I had the students listen to get the main idea and then had the students read the transcript and try to predict which words and phrases would be stressed. After they did this, we listened to the editorial again and the students checked to see if they had correctly predicted which words were stressed. This activity had the added benefits of providing students with language as it was used in the media and of teaching them about topics of interest to the local community. Although I cannot say for certain that the students were able to transfer effective use of stress to their own teaching presentations, they enjoyed the activity and saw that the authentic broadcasts, which had not been altered for language learners, were easy to understand because of the newscaster's speaking style. Both of these experiences made it clear to me that authentic materials need to be used in teaching productive skills as well.

For most teachers, it is easier to see the connection between authentic materials and receptive skills. In contrast, it may not be immediately clear what students should do with authentic materials to promote productive skills. The goal of this chapter is to make some recommendations regarding how authentic materials can be used as the basis for speaking and writing activities.

What the Research Says . . .

There is admittedly little empirical research showing a direct link between the use of authentic materials and improved speaking and writing. In other words, there are few experimental studies comparing groups that have used authentic and non-authentic materials during instruction. For example, Aufderhaar (2004) used radio plays, poetry, and recorded short stories to teach suprasegmentals (i.e., stress and intonation patterns) to international teaching assistants, similar to what I had done. She had students analyze the texts and transcribe portions. The students also recorded themselves reading parts of the texts and comparing their speech to the original. Aufderhaar interviewed the 24 participants in her study and was able to document the students' perception that the use of authentic materials was helpful in learning pronunciation. She did not, however, collect pre- and post-test data and compare the students' speech to that of a control group.

Research comparing groups who do and do not use authentic materials is difficult to design, particularly if the instruction occurs over any extended period. The challenge involves randomly assigning students and keeping all variables except the materials constant. We know of only two experimental studies that are related to the use of authentic materials. Abrams (2014) used a German film to teach pragmatics (i.e., how to use language appropriately in different social settings) to first-year students of German using seven 10- to 15-minute lessons over seven weeks. The control group also watched the film but answered comprehension questions and did not focus on pragmatics. No statistics were done in the small-scale study, but Abrams showed examples from discourse-completion tests in which the treatment group was able to apply some of the strategies from the film such as using mitigating devices to make or reject a request. (Mitigating devices include words or phrases to soften a request such as *I'm sorry*.) In addition, the treatment group showed more awareness of pragmatic rules. This study does not show that authentic materials are superior to non-authentic materials because both groups watched the film. Rather, it shows the effectiveness of authentic materials combined with instruction, and it illustrates how authentic materials can be used even in a first-year class (see Myth 1).

Gilmore (2011) is the only study that we know of that attempted to tease out the effects of materials even though, as mentioned earlier, it is impossible to keep instruction completely constant while changing only the materials. This ambitious study included four intact EFL classes in Japan taught over 10 months. Two classes had the textbook as their main source of input while two received authentic input. Thirteen different measures from eight assessment instruments were used. Of the 13 measures, eight showed greater gains for the experimental group using the authentic materials, five of which were measures on productive tasks including fluency scores and measures of strategic competence (i.e., how speakers use strategies to communicate including gestures or circumlocution). The five measures that did not differ between the two groups were all on productive tasks (e.g., vocabulary subscores from an oral interview). Although this study offers evidence on the effects and limits of authentic materials, it needs to be interpreted cautiously because we cannot be sure which of the results are related to the materials themselves and which are related to the methods used to teach from the materials.

Research from Second Language Acquisition

Because there is so little direct empirical evidence regarding authentic materials and productive skills, we turn to research examining exposure to input and its effect on second language acquisition. There have been several studies that have shown that more exposure to L2 input facilitates language learning; these studies include those comparing study abroad to at-home instruction with regard to gains in speaking and writing (see Llanes & Muñoz, 2013, for a concise and clear review) and studies that compare different amounts of input (e.g., Verspoor & Smiskova, 2012). However, none of these studies consider the amount of authentic language input. For example, students in a study abroad context likely have more access to authentic materials, but they also interact in the target language with interlocutors who modify their speech. Furthermore, with regard to oral skills, there is even some research to suggest that authentic materials alone are not helpful without specific types of instruction (e.g., Pica, 2002, and Darhower, 2014). Nevertheless, we feel that an argument can be made for the benefits of incorporating authentic materials into speaking and writing activities based on tenets of usage-based approaches to second language acquisition.

Usage-based approaches to second language acquisition support the notion that (great quantities of) exposure are essential to learning and that L2 learners, to a certain extent, are sensitive to the frequency of vocabulary and structures. Tyler (2010) discussed different models of usage-based approaches to SLA but summarized what they have in common:

> The central idea in usage-based models is *that a user's language emerges as a result of exposure to numerous usage events* (Kemmer & Barlow, 2000), that is, situated instances of the language user understanding or producing language to convey particular meaning in a specific communicative situation. When a speaker engages in communication, it is assumed that she is attempting to achieve specific interactional goals using intentionally chosen linguistic strategies aimed at members of her speech community. Tying usage events to particular speech communities reflects the understanding that actual language use is culturally and contextually embedded. (p. 271) [emphasis added]

It is precisely this exposure that forms the basis for the use of authentic materials in second language learning. In another review of usage-based approaches, Ellis and Wulff (2015) also state that what the various usage-based approaches have in common is that "learning is primarily based on learners' exposure to their second language (L2) in use, that is, the linguistic input they receive" (p. 74). Furthermore, both Tyler (2010) and Ellis and Wulff (2015) highlight, with reference to empirical studies, that learners are sensitive to frequency information and note that what is more frequent is processed more easily. Verspoor and Smiskova (2012) found that writers who received more input produced more chunks of language. This notion of chunks or formulaic sequences is particularly important because in order to sound more proficient, learners need to be able to use collocations and phrases that are commonly used outside of the classroom. Li and Schmitt (2009) conducted a longitudinal case study of a Chinese graduate student's writing and found that, according to her self-appraisal, more than 40 percent of the student's newly acquired phrases in the U.K. came from her academic reading.

TEACHING SPOKEN LANGUAGE

With regard to spoken language, it has been clearly shown that features used in natural language differ from what it is found in language teaching materials (Carter & McCarthy, in press), and most would agree that learners need some exposure to authentic materials. What is not clear, however, is what teachers should do with these materials in a language class, particularly when the goal is oral communication. Timmis (2005) noted that despite progress in describing spoken grammar, there has been little consensus on how to teach it. Carter and McCarthy (in press) do not develop the idea of how to teach and instead refer back to Timmis (2005), who explains how to analyze authentic oral texts but does not propose any follow-up speaking activities.

Long (2015), in his discussion of task-based language teaching, argues against using authentic materials alone as a basis for teaching speaking because he believes that a task (something one does in life) should be the unit around which a syllabus is created, not a text. He argues that frequency data from authentic texts are not useless but that they are limited. Furthermore, he points out that text analysis activities can be simply grammar and vocabulary exercises that do not fit with his principles of task-based language teaching, which are based on findings from cognitive-interactionist approaches to SLA. This approach explains that students learn by interacting in the target language while trying to understand and be understood. Although we believe text analysis activities, such as those described by Timmis (2005), can benefit some learners, particularly in the area of raising students' awareness of various aspects of language, we agree that more attention should be given to the actual activities students do with the authentic texts.

Long's (2015) book has several clear examples of task-based lesson related to spoken language tasks. One in particular, teaching students how to negotiate a police traffic stop, makes use of discourse from authentic interactions with police. Students listen and deconstruct the speech event (i.e., the traffic stop) with the teacher's help. They read the transcripts and are then given role play cards to which they have to apply what they learned. Although Long argues that authentic materials may be too difficult for low-proficiency students, he explains that it is not simplification of language that is helpful but rather elaboration (for more discussion of this see Myth 6). This elaboration can be built into the materials themselves, at which point they are no longer authentic. Alternatively, the teacher can scaffold while students are working with the authentic material, and this results in another type of elaboration.

Content-based classes, most of which use some or all authentic materials, afford us a context in which to look at language learning with authentic materials. There is an accumulation of evidence from content-based classes that authentic materials alone are not enough to push students' speaking skills. In advanced foreign language classes where authentic materials are used exclusively, speaking skills may not progress. For example, Glisan (2012), in her discussion of the national standards, cited studies showing that teacher talk can dominate advanced classes, giving learners no opportunity to improve their speaking skills. Indeed, Polio and Zyzik (2009) found that among six Spanish literature classes (averaging 23 students per class) where the focus was on literary texts, all the students together produced between

216 and 927 words per 80-minute class. This means that excluding reading aloud, each student produced an average of nine to 40 words in the 80-minute classes.

More recently, Darhower (2014) studied three advanced Spanish literature and culture classes to determine the extent to which the class discussions afforded students the chance to use the language described in the advanced and superior ACTFL guidelines (e.g., narrate in present, past, and future time frames; discuss abstract topics). Interestingly, only one teacher question out of all three sessions was related to the superior functions (*¿Cuáles son los pros y los contras de esa solución?* "What are the advantages and disadvantages of that solution?"). Overall, only 19 percent of the teacher questions were above the intermediate level (i.e., intermediate/advanced, advanced, or superior). Taking a different approach, Pica (2002) examined class discussions from a literature and a culture ESL class in which authentic readings and films were used. Although her examples show some attempts to elicit higher-level discourse functions, the teachers did not focus on language or provide much feedback. Polio and Zyzik (2009) found that teachers did address student errors through recasts (i.e., by repeating the students' utterances with the error corrected) when discussing literature, but there were almost no other attempts made to focus on language in class discussions. Likely, as a result, the students perceived that their speaking skills increased least when compared to skills in listening, reading, writing, grammar, or vocabulary. We see this as further evidence that reading of authentic texts and discussion alone is not enough to improve speaking skills.

Finally, Rodgers (2015) conducted a study that partially replicated the results of Polio and Zyzik (2009). He examined two Spanish and two French content courses in which the instructors used authentic readings, films, and documentaries. His results show that there was little focus on language and that students perceived that their speaking skills improved the least. Rodgers went a step further and tested students on their general proficiency, using a C-test (a test in which students have to fill in blanks in a passage while seeing only the first letter of the word in the blank), and he collected short samples of spoken and written language related to both the class content and the students' lives (e.g., talk about your last vacation). The results need to be interpreted cautiously because of small sample sizes and limited testing, but the results suggest that there was some improvement on overall proficiency and on writing, which can be seen as a positive result. Speaking results showed no significant improvement, and no students improved more than 10 percent. Of course, there was no control group, so we do not know if a group who did not use authentic materials would have performed differently, but this study is an excellent start in helping us understand how language does and does not improve in a class where authentic materials were the basis for listening, reading, and discussion.

To summarize, there is no evidence that authentic materials alone will improve students' speaking proficiency; in fact, most research suggests that students have to use the language to improve their speaking skills. Input is necessary, but not sufficient; in other words, we must have input to learn, but we need more than input. Teachers have to do something with the texts using scaffolding and elaboration techniques, and learners have to be pushed to produce language based on the texts.

TEACHING WRITING

Much of what we have said about speaking can be said about writing, namely that exposure to authentic (written) language is necessary but that appropriate activities need to be done with the texts. Most writing, however, naturally elicits attention to language form, and instructors are more likely to give feedback on written language. The link between reading and writing is also fairly widely acknowledged, so many authors have written about incorporating authentic materials into writing classes. For example, Caplan (2010) described content-based ESL classes using young adult novels and the related writing assignments as an alternative to the five-paragraph essay; in other words, students read to write. Redmann (2005) illustrated the use of a variety of journal writing assignments that can be used in literature classes. Such journal entries give students an opportunity to produce language associated with their reading.

Much has been written about using authentic materials to teach academic writing, particularly to advanced ESL students; there has been much less about teaching students of languages other than English. Generally, this research analyzes specific genres so that language and organizational features of the genres can be taught. Different approaches to analyzing genre exist, but we discuss here the work of Swales (summarized in Swales, 1990, 2005) who has extensively analyzed *rhetorical moves* in academic texts with the goal of teaching these moves and the language used to accomplish them. (An example of a move in an academic journal article would include *establishing a niche*. In an email to a professor, it might include *stating the reason for the email*.) Teaching materials have been based on Swales' analyses of research articles (e.g., Feak & Swales, 2009; Swales & Feak, 2011). Most empirical research, however, is descriptive and does not have a pre- or post-test control group study. Nevertheless, the studies are useful in providing examples of how authentic materials can be used to teach writing.

Myskow and Gordon (2009) reported on an EFL study of Japanese high school EFL students who participated in a genre-based writing lesson involving a university application letter, similar to what would be called a college essay or statement of purpose in a U.S. context. After schema building, the students analyzed the moves in such essays (e.g., write about your academic accomplishments). Myskow and Gordon do not report on evaluation data, but Yasuda (2011), who also worked with EFL students in Japan, conducted a more extensive study of the use of authentic materials to teach a genre, in this case, email. With authentic examples of emails, she created a semester-long curriculum by varying the types of email assignments and conducted a pre- and post-test design to show improvement in the students' writing. She documented quantitative improvements in the students' writing but, again, without a control group, we cannot say for certain that her genre-based approach was better than any other approaches.

A related but different approach has been taken by Byrnes and her colleagues in the Georgetown University German program. Much has been written about this five-year genre-based curriculum including details of the authentic genres used and the accompanying language goals (Byrnes, Maxim, & Norris, 2010). It appears that authentic oral and written texts were used exclusively, except at the beginning level where a textbook was also used. The progression of the students' language use in this program has been written about in a variety of studies, but to give one example, Byrnes (2009) examined the development of students' writing with regard to the use nominalization, a feature of academic writing. Her study concluded that students improved in this area of writing. Ryshina-Pankova (2011), writing about the same program, showed that students improved in their persuasive writing, particularly in the language used to interact with the reader.

Much academic writing involves the skill of writing from sources, which are by definition authentic. There is a huge body of literature on teaching students paraphrasing, citation, and synthesis skills, but this research is beyond the scope of this book as it is specific to academic writing. For those interested in learning more about academic writing from sources, Feak and Swales (2009), which focuses on writing literature reviews, is a good starting point.

We end by discussing corpus-based approaches to teaching writing (in contrast to teaching grammar as discussed in Myth 2). Quinn (2015) described in detail a series of activities for teaching third-year Japanese university EFL learners to use a corpus to interpret feedback. These activities included instructing students on how to use a corpus and asking them to keep logs of their revisions based on their corpus searches. She collected only questionnaire data and noted mostly positive attitudes with the exception of students who found the English interface too difficult despite having received instruction on using the corpus. She supplemented their corpus use with individual teacher student sessions, which suggests that even intermediate-level writers may need assistance in using a corpus to revise their writing. Similarly, O'Sullivan and Chambers (2006), in an action research study, observed 14 students of French as they revised their grammar through use of a corpus after having received a paper where the teacher underlined their grammatical errors. They report positive results in terms of the number of errors that students were able to correct as well as the students' perceived helpfulness of the correction, but they did not provide a comparison of how effective non–corpus based resources were.

In a different type of study, Kennedy and Miceli (2010) described a way to help L2 learners of Italian use a corpus at the pre-writing stage. Students in a fourth-semester Italian class wrote six chapters of an autobiography, with each chapter related to a specific theme. The students began by using a technique they called *pattern-hunting*:

> For example, when the students were writing about their sense of personal space in one of their autobiography chapters, we suggested pattern-hunting in relation to questions such as "What sorts of things might I talk about in relation to my living space?" and "What adjectives or set phrases might I use to talk about my need for space?" Most started by searching on the familiar word *spazio*. This not only turned up ideas and expressions to borrow, such as *reagire di fronte alle invasioni del proprio spazio* ("react to the invasion of one's space"), *ritagliare uno spazio per sé* ("carve out a space for oneself"), and *rubare spazio* ("take space") . . . but also triggered further searches, on words encountered in the concordance lines, such as *percorso* ("path") and *compromesso* ("compromise"). (p. 32)

The point was to generate ideas and language for their essays. This was followed by *pattern-finding*, a more conventional approach that allowed the students to look up, for example, which prepositions followed certain verbs. Through a case study of three students, Kennedy and Miceli (2010) were able to document the kinds of searches that students did as well as their attitudes toward using the corpus during the writing stage. They concluded that two of the students found the corpus quite helpful while one preferred dictionary use.

Despite many studies in which authentic materials are used during writing instruction, most researchers have shown that they are effective in a limited sense—they can raise students' awareness of genres and of grammar and vocabulary. Furthermore, students have mostly positive attitudes toward the materials and corpus tools. More research on student learning needs to be done, and many of these studies could be replicated by adding assessment measures of learning.

What We Can Do . . .

1. Create activities in which students have to do something with the language in authentic texts and not simply understand the language.

Because research has shown that exposure is not enough to help students acquire productive use of language, create activities in which students have to listen or read closely and then have to reproduce some of the language. These can be fairly standard language classroom activities such as dictations or cloze activities, but the difference is that they are created from authentic materials and can serve to direct the students' attention to important aspects that are needed for production. For example, students can read a newspaper article on a specific event with several of the past tense verbs deleted. After students fill in the blanks and the original answers and possible alternatives are discussed, students can be given a related article to read or a related newscast to listen to. The students can then produce an oral or written summary of the text and contrast the first and second texts.

The teacher can also pull out specific sentences from a text for a dictation to focus on specific grammar, vocabulary, or chunks of language. This is best done after the students have read or listened to the text so that they understand the general meaning. There are many variations on dictation including a dictogloss, described in Appendix E, that are preferable to traditional dictation, which often uses isolated or fabricated sentences.

Other options include deleting certain sentences from texts and asking students to write their own possible sentences. More advanced students can be given sentences from the text to paraphrase. The purpose of these activities is both to get students to read closely and to produce language encountered in the text.

2. Analyze authentic language and scaffold difficult texts.

When students read or listen to an authentic text, they may try to get the gist while skipping over difficult language. If students are to truly benefit from authentic texts, teachers need to analyze and scaffold difficult language so that students' attention is drawn to structure, chunks, and vocabulary that students might miss when listening or reading for general comprehension. For example, students could listen to two related National Public Radio stories (e.g., similar but different events or two opinions on the same issue). After a first listening, the teacher can pause at points and focus on difficult or unusual language. Note that the teachers should elaborate (Long, 2015), as opposed to simplify, which some non-authentic texts tend to do. After scaffolding, students can be asked to write an essay contrasting the two stories.

For lower-proficiency students, two simple customer-written online restaurant reviews could be contrasted with the teachers' help. Students could then do a role play in which two friends compare different experiences with the same restaurant based on the reviews.

3. During discussion activities about authentic texts, ask questions that will elicit complex responses and then give language feedback on those responses.

Darhower (2014), as discussed, provides an example in his study of a teacher in a Spanish literature and culture class discussing a painting. He shows how the teachers and students co-construct an analysis, but he notes that most of the students' utterances are one to three words long. One understandable concern is that if teachers ask challenging questions, students might not respond, so then teachers move on to simple questions so that students produce some language. One solution is to give students challenging questions before they are discussed in class. These questions should force students to analyze texts more deeply and to talk about abstract topics. Students will be more likely to respond to difficult questions that they have had time to consider before class. Darhower includes specific questions that can be asked to increase the complexity of students' output.

Even if the students are producing more complex language, research in content-based classes has shown that teachers may not provide feedback during oral discussions. This is presumably because teachers are focused on content and want to keep a discussion going without students' fear of correction. When feedback is given, recasts are often used (see Zyzik & Polio, 2008). Although recasts are helpful, teachers should also sometimes stop and explicitly discuss common vocabulary and grammatical errors that arise; recasts alone do not provide a thorough enough explanation of the issue. If teachers are uncomfortable explicitly correcting students in class, at the end of class, they can ask students to write for ten minutes about the oral discussion and then go over common errors in the next class.

4. Consider genre-based approaches to writing even at the beginning levels.

Much research has shown that genre-based curricula can be successfully implemented while exposing students to authentic language. Beginners will not be able to write or even understand many genres, but lessons can still focus on the reading and production of some genres. Ideally, the genres should be ones that students will have to use in real life, such as email, academic statements, and so on. However, in foreign language contexts where needs are often not clear, a genre-based curriculum allows students to see and analyze authentic language and then produce language. In addition to the email-based lessons discussed earlier, individual lessons using online reviews of products such as clothing could be analyzed and written. We highly recommend reading Byrnes et al. (2010) for a detailed description of using genre across levels. As one example of a genre used at the first year level, they mention recipes. It is easy to see how recipes could be made comprehensible to beginners and that students could be then asked to write their own recipes for their favorite foods. In English, the grammatical structures associated with recipes would include quantifiers and imperatives, so these would be good targets for language-focused instruction. Byrnes et al. also give examples of how topics are recycled throughout the curriculum as students move from easier to more complex genres.

MYTH 6

Modifying or simplifying authentic texts always helps language learners.

In the Real World . . .

I recently finished reading the biography of Sonia Sotomayor, the Supreme Court Justice appointed in 2009. (This is Eve.) Her biography, published in both English (*My beloved world*) and Spanish (*Mi mundo amado*) provides an intimate look into her childhood growing up in the Bronx and the many challenges she faced. As the first Hispanic woman to be appointed to the Supreme Court, it is no wonder that she figures prominently in many Spanish-language textbooks, especially in those that include a chapter on the United States as one of the Spanish-speaking countries. In one of these introductory textbooks (Hershberger, Navey-Davis, & Borrás, 2011), we find the following reading about Sonia Sotomayor (glosses that appear in the textbook are omitted here):

> *Sonia Sotomayor es la primera jueza de origen hispano y la tercera mujer en la Corte Suprema de Justicia de los Estados Unidos. Ella se gradúa con honores de la secundaria en el Bronx, recibe una beca*

*para la Universidad de Princeton donde también **se gradúa** con honores, y finalmente **estudia** Derecho en la Universidad de Yale. Antes de ser jueza de la Corte Suprema, ella **trabaja** exitosamente como abogada y fiscal.* (p. 28)

Sonia Sotomayor is the first female judge of Hispanic origin and the third woman on the Supreme Court of the United States. She graduates with honors from high school, receives a scholarship to Princeton where she also graduates with honors, and finally studies law at Yale University. Before becoming a Supreme Court justice, she works successfully as a lawyer and district attorney.

This is a simplified text that has been written for the novice L2 learner. It provides concrete biographical information in a way that is accessible for the novice learner, using many cognates and high-frequency vocabulary. What is odd about this text is the use of the present tense (see verbs in bold) to relate past events. If we compare this simplified text to a number of authentic texts on the same topic, we find that these events are consistently expressed in the past with the preterit. (I checked a variety of authentic texts published in both the U.S. and Spain and all of them rely on the preterit to express these major life events in Sotomayor's trajectory.)

Now, I don't want to suggest that the use of the present is ungrammatical in past tense contexts. In fact, native speakers of Spanish do use the present tense in narrations about the past, but they do so primarily with verbs that express states (e.g., *to be*) rather than actions that have a clear beginning and end (e.g., *to graduate*). To make matters worse, this particular simplified text mixes two different functions of the present: the present for states that are not limited in time (e.g., Sonia Sotomayor **is** the first female judge of Hispanic origin) and the so-called historical present (e.g., she **receives** a scholarship to attend Princeton). This is perhaps why the text sounds unnatural to the native speaker or even the highly proficient non-native user.

Yet the authors of the textbook have decided to limit themselves to the present tense in the early chapters, presumably to make the texts more comprehensible. But does this actually help language learners? Would learners have been able to understand the text equally well if the verbs had appeared in the preterit (e.g., *se graduó, recibió, estudió,* etc.). Can you simplify an authentic text and still preserve its authenticity? The answers to these questions continue to generate controversy among researchers, materials writers, and teachers. In this chapter, we try to shed light on these issues and provide some viable alternatives to simplifying authentic texts.

What the Research Says . . .

Preliminaries

In this chapter, we will discuss two different ways of modifying an authentic text: simplification and elaboration. The goal of both types of modification is to make the text more comprehensible—that is, more accessible to a wider range of language learners. Before reviewing the research on whether or not these modifications are beneficial for learners, it is useful to define and give concrete examples of both simplification and elaboration.

As the term implies, *simplification* aims to reduce the difficulty of a text by controlling the lexical items and grammatical structures therein. Long (2015) describes simplified texts as having "relatively short utterances or sentences, a limited range of relatively high frequency vocabulary, a low ratio of dependent to main clauses, and a narrow range of syntactic constructions and verb tenses" (p. 250). Many texts come into existence as simplified texts: They are created specifically for L2 learners by materials developers who follow a set of specifications. The classic example of this is a graded reader, which is a simplified text that adheres to a set of pre-defined word lists and structural guidelines. Somewhat different are simplified texts based on an original (authentic) version and re-written for an L2 audience. Most often, texts are simplified using an intuitive approach (Crossley et al., 2012), meaning that authors rely on their subjective experience to determine which linguistic features to include or eliminate. This is precisely what teachers do when they simplify authentic texts based on their personal understanding of what a group of learners is likely to know. Likewise, some websites designed for L2 learners use the intuitive approach to simplify original newspaper articles.

What do simplified texts look like and how do they differ from authentic texts? Some simplified texts are created using traditional readability formulas that cut word and sentence lengths. Longer, complex sentences are often split into two, as illustrated in this example from Allen (2009, p. 594). Compare version A, the original sentence, with the simplified one in B.

> A. The following year, when Mr. Chirac criticized the American preparations for war in Iraq, he was attacked by the media in the U.S. and Britain.
>
> B. In 2003, Mr. Chirac criticized the American preparations for war in Iraq. Television and radio stations in the USA and Britain attacked him for this.

In addition to shortening sentences, texts are simplified by replacing low-frequency words, eliminating or reducing idiomatic language, and modifying particular constructions (e.g., passive voice, phrasal verbs). Simplified texts may also avoid pronominal reference to a certain degree, which has an impact on how noun phrases are distributed in the text. When sentences get shortened, connectives (e.g., *after, because, moreover*) may get sacrificed in the process. Consider this next example, the introductory paragraph from a Spanish graded reader (Miquel & Sans, 2003, p. 6):

> *Hoy es 15 de julio y en Madrid hace mucho calor: 38° de temperatura. Lola entra en su oficina a las nueve y media*

> *de la mañana. Está de mal humor. Le duela una muela y ha*
> *dormido muy mal.*
>
> Today is July 15 and in Madrid it's very hot: 38 degrees.
> Lola enters her office at 9:30 AM. She is in a bad mood.
> She has a toothache and she didn't sleep well.

Although in this case we don't have an authentic rendition for comparison (the graded readers in this series are written specifically for L2 learners of Spanish), note the absence of connectives between the relatively short sentences, meaning that causal relationships must be inferred (presumably she is in a bad mood *because* she has a toothache and didn't sleep well).

In recent years, researchers have been using sophisticated computational tools to examine how simplified texts differ from authentic ones. This line of research is important because it provides empirical evidence regarding the differences between text types, rather than relying on observations from a few isolated examples. Crossley, Louwerse, McCarthy, and McNamara (2007) examined a small corpus of beginner-level ESL simplified texts and compared them to authentic readings that appeared in two textbooks. Crossley and McNamara (2008) replicated the study with a larger corpus of intermediate-level texts. The results of both studies reveal the following major differences:

- Authentic texts contain more causal verbs and particles (e.g, *because, consequently, as a result*). This difference was statistically significant in Crossley et al. (2007), leading the authors to suggest that authentic texts are "better at demonstrating cause-and-effect relationships" (p. 25). The same trend was observed in Crossley and McNamara (2008), although the difference was not statistically significant.
- Authentic texts contain, on average, more logical operators (*or, and, not, if*). When compared to beginner-level simplified texts, authentic texts display more tokens of *if* and more conditional constructions (Crossley et al., 2007).

- Simplified texts have a higher index of lexical co-reference, which means there is more redundancy (overlap) in the ways nouns are expressed (Crossley et al., 2007; Crossley & McNamara, 2008).
- Simplified texts used significantly more frequent and familiar words than authentic texts (Crossley et al., 2007; Crossley & McNamara, 2008).

These results suggest that some of the modifications involved in creating simplified texts affect the natural structure of discourse. For this reason, the issue of using simplified texts remains controversial in both ESL and foreign language teaching circles. Simplified materials have been criticized for providing "stilted, basal-reader type input" (Long, 2007, p. 130) and for being "stilted, repetitive, and dull" (Long, 2015, p. 250). Swaffar (1985) takes issue with simplified texts for being "culturally and linguistically sanitized" (p. 17). As a result, much of the detail and richness of the original text may be lost, altering the content and the author's intended meaning. Claridge (2005) shows this in her comparison of two original literary works with the graded reader simplified versions of each. Specifically, in the case of Edgar Allen Poe's "The Gold Bug," "the author's intent and the information have been significantly altered in the simplification" (Claridge, p. 151). Claridge ultimately defends the use of simplified texts, but acknowledges that some simplifications are not well done (i.e., they don't convey the same meaning as the original).

From a language acquisition perspective, Long (2007, 2015) is strongly opposed to simplification because such materials impede learning by removing features from the linguistic input. In other words, simplified texts do learners a disservice by not exposing them to the very forms they need to make progress. For this reason, Long favors elaboration, which is the process of adding to a text rather than eliminating or reducing potentially difficult items. The additions are meant to increase redundancy and regularity, and provide additional cues to the text's thematic structure (Parker & Chaudron, 1987). A common technique in elaboration is to provide synonyms, examples, or restatements for difficult lexical items, as shown in these examples from Oh (2001). The original version is given in A and the elaborated text in B.

> A. We are less credulous than we used to be. In the nineteenth century, a novelist. . . .
>
> B. We are less credulous than we used to be. We don't easily believe coincidences, or accidental happenings. In the nineteenth century, a novelist. . . .

As shown, elaboration almost always makes a text longer than the original and in many cases it may also render it more linguistically complex. For example, in a study by Yano, Long, and Ross (1994) elaborated texts were found to be 60 percent longer and 16 percent more complex (in terms of words per sentence) than the authentic texts. Similarly, in O'Donnell (2009), the elaborated versions of literary texts increased in length by 65 percent. Nevertheless, it is hypothesized that elaboration actually makes a text easier to process for L2 learners because of the additional support provided. Ross, Long, and Yano (1991, p. 24) believe that elaboration "provides the reader with a second look at terms and concepts and consequently increases the chance that inferencing about them can be stimulated in the reading process" (as cited in O'Donnell, 2009, p. 516).

Elaboration can also involve structural or grammatical modifications to the text. Long (2015) mentions several characteristics including a preference for full noun phrases over pronouns, more frequent use of canonical (i.e., basic or standard) word order, and the addition of intra- and inter-sentential linkers such as *but, so, however, although, therefore, on the other hand, as a result*, and *whereas*. According to Long (2015), these kinds of modifications are comparable to those made spontaneously by native speakers when interacting with non-native speakers (e.g., foreigner talk). For Long, the crucial advantage of elaboration (over simplification) is that it improves the comprehensibility of input without removing the difficult or unknown items that stimulate language acquisition.

Although simplification and elaboration have been described here as fundamentally different processes, the distinction between them can sometimes become blurred. Some authors consider elaboration to be a type of simplification (cf. Crossley, Yang, & McNamara, 2014). Interesting examples are found in Allen (2009), who analyzed the distribution of relative clauses in simplified news texts and found that, in some cases, the authors added information to make relationships more explicit. Consider the original version given in A and the modified text shown in B (Allen, 2009, p. 594):

A. Enzo Baldoni, kidnapped while travelling

B. Enzo Baldoni, who was kidnapped while travelling

In this example, the additional element expands the participle clause with the intent of making it less elliptical and thus presumably easier to comprehend. Allen found that at the elementary level, "many RCs [relative clauses] have been created by the authors for simplification purposes" (p. 593). Technically speaking, we would consider these types of additions under the rubric of elaboration since material is being added. The point is that in practice, especially in the intuitive approach to modifying texts, both simplification and elaboration may occur concurrently.

To conclude this section, we want to highlight that authentic texts cannot be modified without losing some degree of their authenticity. As Oh (2001) states, "any kind of modification will most likely mask, to a greater or lesser degree, some characteristic features of unmodified input" (p. 91). We are not saying that only authentic texts should be used for language teaching (see the Epilogue for a detailed discussion of this issue). Yet we want the reader to be aware that modifying texts, either via simplification or elaboration, will compromise their authenticity. Even elaboration, which is supposed to retain features of genuine or authentic texts, can distort canonical discourse patterns. Consider the case of subject pronouns in languages like Spanish, which is mentioned by Long (2007) in his description of elaboration. In Spanish, null subjects (subject deletion) are clearly the preferred form, being more frequent than overt pronouns or full noun phrases; the general tendency is to use a null subject to indicate subject continuity, that is, when there is no change of referent. Yet consider the example of elaboration from O'Donnell (2009); additional overt subjects, shown here in brackets [ ], were added to the original text.

> *Los 160 trabajadores del Banco de Ahorros y Préstamos acordaron en gastar todos sus ahorros para comprar conjuntamente medio millón de dólares en números de la lotería de la Florida que subía su pozo acumulado minuto a minuto. [...] [Los empleados] Ponían todas sus esperanzas en el premio gordo para combatir así los rumores de que en pocas semanas [el banco y los empleados] iban a ser absorbidos por el Banco Interamericano y posiblemente [ellos] quedarían en la calle.*

The resulting text, although more explicit about who the subject of each sentence is, creates a discourse pattern that deviates from native Spanish. Furthermore, it begs the question of whether these additions actually help learners in the long run; when the input is elaborated to include more explicit mentions of the subject, learners no longer need to process the verbal cues to sentence interpretation (note that the plural-marked verbs *ponían* and *quedarían* in this example can only refer to the 160 workers mentioned at the beginning of the text). This example of elaboration echoes Long's (2015) concerns with respect to simplification—that a simplified text may improve comprehensibility "at the expense of *language learning*, which is the real goal" (p. 251, emphasis original).

Beyond long-term effects on the language acquisition process, most teachers are rightly concerned with the immediate goal of having learners comprehend a text presented to them. Will altering the text guarantee better comprehension? The research on this issue has yielded somewhat mixed results, which we examine in the next section.

Empirical Studies

An overview of the research shows that simplifying a written text some-times leads to increased comprehension. It does not always lead to bet-ter comprehension because reading is a complex process affected by a number of variables, including but not limited to: the learner's reading proficiency; the learner's background knowledge or familiarity with the topic; text length; and text type (e.g., expository, narrative, argumenta-tive). In other words, when some of these variables are considered in the research design, the effects of text simplification become less obvi-ous or less noticeable.

Young (1999) asked a group of language teachers and linguists to simplify four articles in Spanish on various topics. The approach to simplification was intuitive, that is, the teachers were asked to "sim-plify the text to make it more comprehensible to second-year university level learners" (p. 352). Interestingly, a high percentage of the modifi-cations, ranging from 42 to 59 percent, were lexical in nature. Subsequently, the authentic and simplified versions of these texts were presented to several groups of learners whose comprehension was assessed using both free recall and multiple choice questions. The results indicate that, on average, learners recalled more from the authentic texts than from the simplified versions (free recall). This was true for three of the four articles. A detailed analysis of these recalls indicates that learners understood the main idea of the articles regard-less of whether the text had been simplified or not. In contrast, learners scored higher on the multiple choice test after reading the simplified versions of three of the four texts, although the differences were not significant. Young concludes that text simplification may not be neces-sary if students are "reading a text for comprehension, for the general idea, or for important information" (p. 361). She further suggests that longer texts may be poor candidates for simplification since they natu-rally provide more redundancy and repetition. In sum, the benefits of simplification in Young's study were inconsistent since comprehension scores varied according to the content of the article and type of assess-ment measure (recall versus multiple choice).

There is some evidence that too much simplification can actually be detrimental to the reading process. This is what Tweissi (1998) concluded after comparing ESL learners' comprehension of four versions of a simplified text. The learners who read the fully simplified version (with most parts of the text simplified lexically and syntactically) performed significantly worse than the group of learners who read a lexically simplified version. Thus, although there was a positive effect for simplification overall, Tweissi explained that excessive simplification "might have rendered the fully-simplified text significantly different from normal English in the areas of information distribution and organization and so impeded comprehension" (p. 200). Tweissi's study suggests that lexical simplification alone might be the most effective way of boosting learners' comprehension.

A more recent study by Crossley, Yang, and McNamara (2014) investigated the effect of simplification on text processing (i.e., reading speed) and text comprehension. The authors also considered the participants' overall language proficiency as measured by the TOEFL®, their reading proficiency, background knowledge, and the degree of text simplification (authentic versus intermediate-level versus beginning-level). They selected news texts that had been simplified for language learning purposes. The results indicate that beginning-level simplified texts were read faster and comprehended better than the intermediate-level and authentic texts. No significant differences in reading time or comprehension were found between the intermediate-level and authentic texts. To appreciate the complete picture of the results, however, we must consider the individual differences among the participants. Crossley et al. (2014) show that differences in reading time (speed of processing) were cancelled out by reading proficiency. In other words, reading times are better explained by learners' reading proficiency than the nature of the text. Likewise, comprehension scores interacted with learners' overall language proficiency, with a large difference in comprehension on authentic texts between learners with high and low TOEFL® scores (see Figure 6.1).

Whereas there is barely any difference between groups on the simplified texts, note the large gap between the low and high TOEFL®

Figure 6.1: Reading Comprehension Scores of High- and Low-Scoring TOEFL® Groups

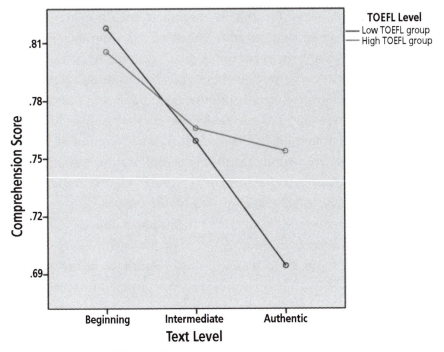

Source: Crossley et al., 2014, p. 106.

groups on the authentic texts. The authors explain that "L2 readers with stronger language proficiency were better able to cope with the linguistic challenges of authentic text" (p. 107). Furthermore, background knowledge was an important factor in the comprehension of the authentic texts. As expected, those with higher background knowledge comprehended the authentic texts better than readers with less background knowledge. Crossley et al. (2014) conclude that students who have higher language proficiency and/or higher background knowledge are better served by authentic texts, which push them to generate inferences and connect ideas.

The importance of background knowledge was confirmed by Keshavarz, Atai, and Ahmadi (2007), who showed that the content of a text has a greater effect than linguistic simplification. Their participants read content-familiar and content-unfamiliar passages in various forms: in the original and in lexically and/or syntactically simplified versions. Across the board, the performance on the content-familiar text was better than on the content-unfamiliar one. In contrast, there was no main effect for simplification, meaning that simplified passages were not understood better than the original versions. Yet, there was an interesting interaction between content and simplification; specifically, lexical simplification facilitated comprehension and recall of the content-unfamiliar reading passage. Keshavarz et al. (2007) explain that when content is unfamiliar to the reader, unknown vocabulary is more difficult to guess from context, and thus simplification has a positive effect. Conversely, when the content is familiar to the reader, there seems to be no added benefit from simplifying the text.

Given the inconclusive results for text simplification, perhaps elaboration really is a better option. Oh (2001) conducted a study to compare the effects of simplification and elaboration on reading comprehension. Korean high school students, grouped into two proficiency groups (high and low), read texts in either the baseline, simplified, or elaborated condition. The simplified texts contained shorter sentences, fewer embedded clauses, and fewer low-frequency words. In contrast, the elaborated texts were longer than the baseline and simplified texts because of the added redundancy (e.g., examples, paraphrases, synonyms). Participants' comprehension of the texts was measured with multiple choice questions that targeted general, specific, and inferential comprehension. Oh's results indicate that overall there were no significant differences between the two types of modification. Nevertheless, some differences emerge when considering proficiency level. The lower proficiency group did not perform better when reading simplified texts compared to the baseline condition. In contrast, they seemed to benefit from elaboration despite the increased length and complexity of the passages. Finally, the general comprehension of the low-proficiency group was poor regardless of the type of text they read, which suggests that no type of modification helped them extract the main idea of each passage. Oh ultimately argues in favor of elaboration as a better option since it maintains more native-like qualities of the original text, yet the quantitative results don't reveal a major advantage for elaboration over simplification.

O'Donnell (2009) explored the effects of elaboration on literary texts in Spanish. Working with three authentic texts, O'Donnell created elaborated versions that targeted 18 potentially difficult vocabulary words in each text. It should be noted that the authentic versions were taken from the students' textbook, which contained glosses in the margins. O'Donnell measured student performance in terms of comprehension of the passages and recognition of particular vocabulary words. Comprehension was assessed with an immediate recall protocol (i.e., write in English as much as you can recall about the text you just read). Vocabulary recognition was tested via a simple Spanish-English translation task. The results of the study are somewhat difficult to interpret because of the nature of the comprehension test. Participants who read the elaborated versions of the texts produced significantly longer recalls for two of the three texts. However, it could be argued that students recalled more simply because they read more (note that the elaborated texts were 65 percent longer than the authentic versions). In terms of vocabulary recognition, there was a positive effect for reading the elaborated versions, but it was significant for only one of the texts. When we compare the effects of glossing versus elaboration, there appears to be no difference. Specifically, readers recognized 29.65 percent of the words that were glossed (in the authentic version) and 30.27 percent of the words that were elaborated. One way to interpret this finding is that elaboration, which provides definitions, synonyms, or paraphrases, is a type of in-text glossing. O'Donnell suggests that elaboration "might serve to keep the readers' attention within the body of the text" (p. 528). O'Donnell concludes that elaboration be viewed as viable option for working with literary texts but also raises a number of concerns such as knowing where and how to elaborate a text and the time involved in producing the elaborated version.

Is it possible to make a text more comprehensible without resorting to some type of modification? One viable solution is proposed in Van den Branden (2000), who studied the effects of negotiation of meaning as an alternative to text modification. Van den Branden's study was carried out in the Dutch context with a heterogeneous sample of primary school students, many of whom (39 percent) were nonnative speakers from immigrant backgrounds. The students read a detective story and answered a set of comprehension questions that accompanied each chapter. The experiment was set up in such a way that all students engaged in the four treatment conditions during the course of reading the story: (1) unmodified input; (2) modified (simplified and elaborated) input; (3) collective negotiation; and (4) pair negotiation. The results show that negotiation of meaning (in both collective and pair formats) yielded significantly higher comprehension scores than unmodified and modified input. In addition, negotiation of meaning provided more uniform results, benefitting students of all proficiency levels. In contrast, the effects of modified input were most favorable for students who already had relatively high language proficiency. Van den Branden concludes that negotiation of meaning is a way for comprehension problems to "come to the surface" (p. 438) and eventually get solved, especially in heterogeneous classrooms.

The research we have reviewed in this chapter shows that the effects of simplification and/or elaboration are complex and not easily predictable. It is *not* the case that simplification always leads to enhanced comprehension of a written text. In fact, even for lower-proficiency learners (who we might expect to benefit the most from simplification), we find somewhat inconsistent results. Recall that in Crossley et al. (2014), authentic texts were particularly challenging for lower-proficiency learners; these same learners benefitted from text simplification, scoring highest on the passages simplified to the beginner level (see Figure 6.1). However, in Oh (2001), the lower-proficiency learners scored poorly on general comprehension questions regardless of the type of text they read (simplified, elaborated, or baseline). One point that researchers can agree on is that external modification interacts with numerous factors such as learners' proficiency level, their reading ability, their background knowledge, and even the type of questions we use to assess comprehension.

From a pedagogical perspective, an important consideration is the time required in simplifying and/or elaborating a text. If only a few low-frequency words are replaced with more familiar words, then the time investment may not be unreasonable. However, re-writing a text with a large number of structural modifications (e.g., shortening sentences, eliminating subordinate clauses) will necessarily require more time. O'Donnell (2009) mentioned the time involved in text modification as a potential disadvantage; she explained that after the first round of modifications, two native Spanish speakers read the texts to identify points in which the language seemed "forced" (p. 518), leading to a second round of modifications. For teachers, the time investment must be balanced with the return: If modifying a text does not lead to much better comprehension, then perhaps working with the authentic text— with appropriate scaffolding for the students—may be more efficient.

What We Can Do . . .

1. Consider working with authentic texts when learners have a good deal of background knowledge about the topic.

This point is made very well by Crossley et al. (2014), who conclude that "authentic texts may be particularly useful if the content is relatively familiar to the students" (p. 108). Background knowledge may compensate for the challenging nature of the authentic text. One reason for this is that knowing something about a topic usually entails already having some of the vocabulary to talk about it. In the case of a narrative, being familiar with the content or major events of a story will boost comprehension. For example, think about reading a book based on a movie that you've already seen or vice-versa. Bernhardt (2011) suggests that students be given the opportunity to engage their first-language literacy by reading about topics in their L1 and anticipating key vocabulary that they will need to discuss the content/issue in the foreign language. This is an excellent way of preparing students to read authentic texts in the target language, but certainly not the only one (see Myth 4 for additional ideas).

2. Consider using unmodified, authentic texts for the purposes of intensive reading.

The purpose of reading is important as we decide what kind of texts to present to students. Extensive reading involves reading a lot of material that is easy and thus enjoyable to read (Day & Bamford, 1998). One of the main goals of extensive reading is to increase reading fluency, which is characterized by automatic and accurate processing of the words on a page. If the goal is to build fluency, learners are probably better served by modified materials (e.g., graded readers) that allow them to read large amounts of text without stopping to look up words in the dictionary. In contrast, the goal of intensive reading is quite different, with the focus being on slow, deliberate reading of texts that require attention to language features in order to be understood. Allen (2009) suggests that authentic texts be used for intensive reading since the goal is to study the language (i.e., lexis, grammar, discourse features) in context. Furthermore, intensive reading is generally facilitated by the teacher, meaning that various types of support—linguistic and otherwise—can be provided to the students as they make sense of the text.

3. Instead of simplifying texts, direct students to focus only on particular sections or certain paragraphs of an authentic text.

This technique can work well for informational texts. For example, number the paragraphs in a newspaper article and tell students to focus on the information in Paragraphs 1, 2, and 4. Guide students to do an intensive reading of these selected paragraphs rather than shortening the text or simplifying the language. The more motivated students or those with better language skills may go back and read the entire text, thereby gaining an additional benefit. Note that this technique will not necessarily work for all genres of text. Likewise, be careful that the omitted sections do not contain key information that is referenced in the paragraphs you've assigned.

4. Distinguish between simplification that affects the syntax/discourse of the text and lexical simplification.

This is an important point that stems from research that confirms the massive amount of vocabulary needed to read authentic texts without assistance. Nation (2006) concluded that learners need to know about 8,000–9,000 word families in order to read independently, with the assumption that one needs to know 98 percent of the running words in the text. Even if we consider lower levels of coverage (95 percent, for example), this still entails knowing about 4,000 word families (Uden, Schmitt, & Schmitt, 2014). Given these estimates, vocabulary researchers generally recommend the use of simplified texts for the purpose of extensive reading. Along the same lines, some researchers advocate for lexical simplification while preserving the original sentence structure. For example, Gardner and Hansen (2007) explain that "judicious lexical simplification allows most of the syntactic and discourse structures of a text to remain untouched, thus preserving most of the natural cohesiveness of unaltered originals" (p. 42). For teachers who decide they must simplify a text, a more conservative approach would call for lexical simplification only. We concur with Tweissi (1998) in that "when amount of simplification is brought into play, it is more likely that the less the better" (p. 201).

For learners to benefit from using authentic texts, the associated tasks must also be authentic.

In the Real World . . .

In the introduction to this book, we used the example of a restaurant menu. English menus in North America look very different from one another depending on the type of cuisine and cost of the restaurant. They are often visually appealing and may contain colloquial or specialized vocabulary. Fabricated menus in language textbooks often look nothing like real menus, use simple vocabulary, and lack anything other than stereotypical cultural information (e.g., Americans eat hot dogs.). When teaching the ESL practicum with graduate students, I have seen students bring in some interesting realia that they have collected to use in lessons. (This is Charlene.) One student brought in a glossy menu from IHOP full of tempting pictures of whipped cream-covered pancakes, and one brought in a menu from the famous Zingerman's delicatessen in Ann Arbor (Michigan) that included phrases like *applewood-smoked bacon* and *challah French toast*. They were great cultural artifacts that illustrated the wide range of food choices one could find within Michigan, but no one knew what to do with the menus. The master's students understood that giving their ESL students a list of words to memorize would not lead to retention of the words, as discussed in Myth 4, and they rightly questioned whether or not ESL students needed to know words like *challah*. Because of these issues, no one really knew what pedagogical task should be associated the menus even though we all knew what the real-life task was: to get food to eat. In real life, we could point to the food on the menu at IHOP. At Zingerman's, we could order the challah French toast based on our knowledge of the word *toast* and hope that challah was not some kind of meat. In the end, we did not solve the problem of what to do with all the new vocabulary from the menu, but we had a good discussion about the relationship between the materials and the associated task.

In the case of the menu, an authentic task might be a role play. Students could be given role cards to use with the menus that include statements about dietary restrictions. This task might be authentic for students playing the customer but not necessarily for those playing the waiter unless they had plans to work as a waiter. Furthermore, gestures that could result in obtaining food during the role play may not be pragmatically appropriate, or they may circumvent the students' goals related to language learning. Although role plays, without a doubt, have benefits, pedagogical activities using authentic materials need not be limited to tasks that mimic real world uses of those materials. We discuss reasons that teachers might not want to limit their students to authentic tasks and highlight some studies that examine learning with the use of non-authentic tasks.

What the Research Says . . .

In the introduction, we mentioned Willis's (2004) and Van den Branden's (2006) views that tasks are something with an outcome or a goal to achieve. Skehan's (1998) view of a task is that it has some type of real-world relationship, and Long (2015) sees a task as something that is actually done in real life. We focus here on Ellis's (2000) discussion of *task* versus *exercise*, which he bases on Skehan (1998). Ellis, too, explains that a task has some obvious relationship to an activity in the real world. By this definition, a role play could be considered a task, albeit one that does not necessarily have an outcome unless the role play is structured so that students have a clear problem to solve. An exercise, on the other hand, is seen as something to be completed to learn language that might be needed in a future task; it has no clear communicative goal. (The example of underlining pronouns from Paesani, 2005, in Myth 2 would be an example of an exercise.) In the menu example, an exercise might include some type of vocabulary matching exercise to help students learn the words on the menu. An exercise most definitely does not resemble a real-life activity, whereas a task may resemble a real-life activity in varying degrees or in different ways. For example, the role play looks very much like a real-life activity. Other tasks, as Ellis points out, simply elicit discourse that is similar to what might occur in real life. Consider an information gap activity in which each person has an incomplete map and they need to communicate to find certain locations. The activity itself is not something we would do in real life, but the language used during the activity might be similar to what one would use while asking directions. We could call this a *pedagogic task* to distinguish it from an exercise.

We argue in this chapter that both *exercises* and what might be considered *non-authentic tasks*, or pedagogic tasks, need to be used with authentic materials. We made the point in discussing Myth 5 that input from authentic language alone is not sufficient for learning; students need to do something with the language. This applies to all aspects of language—vocabulary and chunks of language, grammar, and pragmatics. We discuss and describe studies that show that learners need some activity beyond how they would use language in a real-life context and have organized the discussion according to different aspects of language. We then focus on the use of different modalities (i.e., oral vs. written) in language learning activities with authentic materials and argue even the modality of the pedagogic task need not match the modality of the real-life task; varying and combining modalities may facilitate the learning of language found in the authentic materials. As with some of the other issues related to the use of authentic texts, there is no empirical research that directly compares types of tasks with authentic materials to see what leads to greater learning, so we have had to draw on many studies that do not use authentic materials.

Focus on Vocabulary

The discussion in Myth 3 focused on the importance of repetition in learning incidental vocabulary. Another study of repetition is Webb, Newton, and Chang (2013), who had EFL students in Taiwan read and listen to graded (i.e., non-authentic) readers using four different versions of a text. In the control version, students read the text and encountered 18 targeted verb-noun collocations (e.g., *to face facts, to break one's silence*) once. In the other groups, students encountered the targeted verb-noun combination 5, 10, or 15 times. The authors used a series of tests to measure how the number of exposures was related to learning the form and meaning of the collocations in terms of both understanding and producing the collocations. For example, to test the students' receptive knowledge of meaning, the students had to translate a phrase from the text into Chinese. Webb et al. found that on all tests, students' performance improved as the number of exposures increased, but 15 exposures was not necessarily better than 10 exposures. Unfortunately, they were not able to test for delayed effects because of the challenges in doing research on incidental learning; giving a test can draw learners' attention to the vocabulary to be learned for delayed tests.

There are several interesting points about this study that are related to our discussion of what types of tasks to do with authentic materials. First, the reading was from a graded reader, so the students likely did not have to contend with challenging grammar and additional vocabulary while reading for meaning. If the students did not learn new words well with only one encounter in a graded reader, they will certainly need more explicit attention to new vocabulary in a more difficult text. Second, the students learned better with multiple exposures, which may not occur in short readings; many short, interesting authentic texts do not repeat vocabulary words ten times. Furthermore, when we think about what real-world task is associated with reading a short story or news article, there may not be one beyond reading for pleasure. In other words, if students read an authentic story or news article, the associated authentic task (e.g., chatting with a friend about the story) may not lead to vocabulary learning unless there are multiple repetitions of the word. Finally, Webb et al. (2013) had students listen and read at the same time, and this is likely never an authentic task. (See the discussion of audio-assisted reading in Myth 3.) This study suggests if we want students to learn vocabulary faster and without multiple repetitions, we might want to add an acitivty, or what Ellis (2000) calls an exercise, that focuses on vocabulary. Such an activity could be something like a cloze activity: Before students read, they are given a passage from which words have been deleted and they have to try to predict what word goes in the blank. This activity will help students focus on the new words before they read for meaning.

In Myth 4, we mentioned the work of Laufer and Hulstijn (2001) who stressed that that learner engagement with the new words and a need to understand the new word in the associated task will lead to better retention of the word. They used the term *task-induced involvement*. An authentic task might not create the necessary involvement needed to learn a new word. In the Webb et al. (2013) study, we think that the students learned more by listening and reading at the same time. Webb et al. had students read and listen at the same time for research design purposes, namely so that all students would spend the same amount of time on reading. We believe, however, that here are also learning benefits of this activity, which are discussed in Myth 3. In sum, while read-and-listen activities might not reflect what we do in real life with authentic materials, they may lead to more efficient language learning.

Focus on Grammar

With regard to the teaching of grammar (but also pronunciation and vocabulary), there is a long history in the field of second language acquisition of debate related to what is needed for language learning to occur. These discussions were the basis of the interaction approach. (See review in Gass, 1997.) The idea was that input alone did not inform learners of what they could not say in the target language (Long, 1996). For example, in English, learners might hear several nouns that can be both count and non-count (e.g., *experience*), so they might not know which nouns can never be non-count (e.g., *research*). Long argued that learners need some type of feedback when they produce language. He argued that implicit feedback in the form of communication breakdowns (e.g., *I'm sorry, but I don't understand*) and recasts (learner utterances with the error corrected) were best and that these occurred as learners negotiated meaning trying to understand one another. The facilitative effect of this type of feedback has been supported by several studies (e.g., Mackey, 1999), which raises the question of which classroom tasks can be done with authentic materials that will generate feedback on language and encourage students to negotiate to create meaning in the target language.

Research has shown that certain types of oral tasks will generate more implicit attention to language through interlocutor negotiation (Pica, Kanagy, & Falodun, 1993). In other words, learners will try to understand and be understood more in certain task types. Pica et al. explained in their review of studies that information gap and jigsaw activities (terms often used interchangeably in other studies) most often led to the type of learner modification in language production that we would hope for in oral communication tasks. For example, upon being misunderstood because of a pronunciation problem, a learner may self-correct. Information gap and jigsaw activities are those in which participants have different information and must communicate or exchange information to complete a task; the classic example is a spot-difference task in which each speaker has a similar but different picture and they have to find the differences by talking to one another. For some types of authentic materials, we can easily devise information gap activities that elicit language used in real-life situations even though the actual information gap activity is something we would not do in real life. For example, students can be given real maps with different parts deleted. They will then ask each other for directions to the missing locations on their maps. Alternatively, one person might have a train schedule and the other person has to find out what times he or she can leave to depart for another city. For other types of authentic materials, an information gap activity might be even further removed from real life in that the discourse generated serves the purpose of language learning and does not resemble what is used in authentic communication; we provide examples in the next section.

Despite some agreement that information gap activities were helpful, Pica (1994) cogently argued that even with tasks that encouraged negotiation, negotiation over certain grammatical structures was rare. For example, with regard to grammar, learners are more likely to work and modify their language related to syntactic problems like relative clauses than, for example, third-person singular morphemes. Sato (1990) showed that learners having a conversation, an authentic task, were able to use adverbs to successfully communicate while omitting verb endings that would indicate tense (e.g., *I go to the movies yesterday*). In addition, Swain (1985) and others found that students in French-Canadian immersion programs were not achieving native-like competence in the area of grammar despite listening and interacting in French in their classes. Sato studied two children learning English through conversation (a real-life activity), and the Canadian students were using French in their content courses (also a real-life activity). This study led to discussion of the role of salience and the role of explicit instruction, both of which we can consider when creating tasks to use with authentic texts.

One issue that has long been discussed in the SLA literature is that of salience, how noticeable something is. This concept is related to L1 learning as well; children will first learn syllables, forms, and words that are more salient in the input via stress or sentence position. Pica (2002) showed how the negotiation of oral language could highlight normally less salient features of language through stress or placement in an utterance (e.g., *Put it on the box* could be changed to <u>*On*</u> *the box; Put it* <u>*on*</u> *the box* if a student did not understand. The preposition *on* is more salient in the rephrasing.). In addition, there is growing evidence that explicit instruction can facilitate language learning, beginning with Norris and Ortega's (2000) meta-analysis and continuing to be supported for many, but not all, structures. We also know that certain features such as bound morphemes or aspectual distinctions tend to be universally difficult (DeKeyser, 2005) and thus are less likely to be learned incidentally.

Focus on Pragmatics

Pragmatics can be a difficult area in which to use authentic materials, in part, because, for oral language, it can be difficult to find texts that target what needs to be taught. We also need to consider what types of tasks will facilitate the learning of sometimes subtle pragmatic features. We mentioned Abrams (2014) in Myth 5, who used film to raise students' metalinguistic awareness. In that study, she had students analyze pragmatic features and create dialogues. Although the students' awareness was raised, Abrams noted that her activities did not always lead to correct use. Some pragmatic features are particularly difficult to learn without some kind activity that focuses learners' attention on the features.

Takimoto (2008) summarized the research showing that explicit instruction in pragmatics is helpful. He investigated what type of instruction would help EFL students in Japan learn various types of downgraders that can be used to soften requests. Downgraders include lexical items like *please* but also the more challenging aspectual and tense modifications (e.g., *I was wondering* vs. *I wonder*). In his study,

Takimoto assigned students to one control group and three treatment groups. The three treatment groups received different types of instruction. In the deductive group, the teacher provided explicit instruction and then students had to read contrived dialogues and predict an appropriate request before listening to confirm their choice (also called structured input in this study). The problem-solving group compared dialogues and discussed the relationship between participants and the politeness of the requests. The inductive instruction group received only the structured input activity. All groups learned the targeted structures better than the control group, but the explicit instruction group, unlike in many other studies of language learning, did not do any better and, in fact, did a little worse than the other groups on a delayed post-test.

We want to focus on the structured input tasks and the problem-solving tasks because we feel that these could be used with authentic texts. In the structured input task, students had to read and understand the dialogues. At certain points, there were two similar alternatives with one being more pragmatically appropriate. Students had to choose one and then listen to the dialogue and determine if their choice was correct or not. Such an activity could be used with any type of authentic text. In the problem-solving activity, students were given dialogues between participants with different social statuses in different contexts. Students then had to fill out a sheet highlighting the roles and contextual issues in relationship to the language used in the requests. Again, such an activity could be used with movie or television excerpts in which the same person is seen interacting with, for example, their friend or their boss.

Barbieri (2015) conducted a study on pragmatic discourse features found in U.S. university classes. This study is relevant because it highlights features that appear in authentic discourse that learners may not notice. She studied what are called involvement markers. These markers are related to "the speaker's emotional participation in the ongoing exchange or in their own talk" (p. 153) and, in a sense, show how speakers interact with their audience. They include questions, stance adverbs (e.g., *surprisingly*, *honestly*), intensifiers, confirmation checks, and several others. She looked at a wide range of classroom types and content areas and concluded that North American classroom discourse is highly involved. What is striking is that many of the features of involvement are not terribly salient including intensifiers (*so, too*), linking adverbs (*anyhow*), and downgraders (*kind of, sort of*). One particularly interesting marker was the quotative *like* (e.g., *He was **like**, I'm not doing this anymore*). Given the importance of these markers in understanding the speakers' relationship with the participants, it might be helpful to draw learners' attention to them through some type of activity. Simply listening to lectures and taking notes, an authentic activity, may not highlight important pragmatic features. Activities such as those from Takimoto (2008) could be used. Learners could be given transcripts from real lectures and try to predict possible involvement markers before listening to the lecture. As they listened, they could then check whether or not their predictions were correct.

Nguyen (2013) studied the effects of pragmatics instruction on Vietnamese EFL students' use of modifiers or downgraders when providing constructive criticism to their peers. She conducted a study using a control group, who received no instruction, and a treatment group who received ten 45-minute instructional sessions in the context of providing peer feedback on writing. The instruction included listening to native speakers give feedback and then having the students rate the level of directness of the criticism. The students also had to take sample criticisms and soften them. In addition, after they provided feedback to their peers, they had to listen to the peer feedback sessions and reflect on their language use while critiquing their peers. Nguyen found, through the use of various assessments, that the instruction group performed better than the control group. Using downgraders to soften criticism is difficult, and it is a feature that learners may not notice in natural speech. Therefore, simply having students do a task such as a role play may not result in learning; instead language awareness tasks, such as rating the level of directness, may be needed for learning to occur.

The Use of Different Modalities

The research suggests that learners need to do more with the language from authentic texts than they might do in real life. It might also mean that teachers might need to change the modality of the task to help learners. Earlier in this chapter and also in Myth 3, we mentioned audio-assisted reading, and it is easy to see the benefits of this dual modality (written and aural) task: The written words help learners segment a sentence into words and see new words while letting them hear the sounds and speed up their reading. Similarly, written activities have the potential for facilitating second language acquisition, and this idea has been discussed extensively in the literature (see Williams, 2012, for an overview of the related SLA research). By writing, students can pay more attention to language because the process is slower, giving them more time to tap into explicit knowledge. Also, accuracy of grammar is generally more important in writing than is speaking. Swain (2005) argued in particular for collaborative writing, citing several studies that showed how learners focus on language as they write together. Kowal and Swain (1997) used dictoglosses to get students to reconstruct texts together. In a dictogloss, students listen to a passage several times and take notes. In pairs, they try to reconstruct the passage. In doing so, the students indeed focus on language but also are likely to try new grammar and vocabulary that were part of the passage and that are beyond what they could normally not produce without input. Dictoglosses are a good example of a pedagogic activity that is not an authentic task. They are ideal to use with authentic texts because they require students to try to reproduce language that may beyond their level.

Prince (2013) conducted an exploratory study of variations on dictoglosses to teach listening. Although others have studied dictoglosses, they investigated them in the context of having students work together to reconstruct a passage after listening. Prince, instead, tried to understand how the different variations affected learning. In Appendix G, we show an example of a dictogloss with chunks of language highlighted, but Prince looked at additional variations. In one variation, he asked students to choose one key word from each sentence to write as they listened; students could not take notes beyond the word. After they listened a second time, they could write more. The idea was that students would link more of the incoming language to the words they wrote and thus form chunks. The second variation was to have students listen only once so that they would listen for the main ideas and not individual words. The third variation was to use a passage with unknown low-frequency words and encourage students to use an easier word that might make sense in the context. Although Prince did not conduct an experimental study, he provided many examples and some quantitative data suggesting that these variations helped learners use both top-down and bottom-up listening skills. He also makes the point that authentic materials were not used in his study, but that this is an area for further research. We believe that these variations could all be used with authentic texts at an appropriate level for the students.

One final example of a non-authentic task is Wang and Wang's (2014) study of a story continuation activity. In their study, Chinese EFL students read a story and continued it in two conditions. In a repeated designs study (one in which all students participate in both conditions), the students read a story both in English and in Chinese and continued the story in English. Based on a particular theoretical framework, Wang and Wang reasoned that students would use vocabulary from the English version and make fewer errors in the English condition. In other words, they tested whether or not the students would align their written texts with the English text they had read. In fact, they found that the students produced fewer errors in continuing the English version than the Chinese version. In addition, they used more keywords from the story. (Keywords are words that appear relatively frequently in a text when compared to a general corpus.) Although it appears that the researchers used a non-authentic text, their story continuation activity could easily be used with authentic texts. Moreover, it is a good example of how input from authentic texts can help students use better and more advanced language.

To summarize our understanding of the research, many studies have shown that limiting language use to real-life tasks may not lead to efficient language learning. Certain features of language need to be made salient through interactive activities or explicit instruction. This can be achieved through some of the pedagogic activities surveyed in this chapter including, but not limited to dictogloss, information gap, story continuation, and dual modality activities.

What We Can Do . . .

1. Create activities that encourage students to use the new language from authentic texts even if those activities would not normally be used with such texts.

In real life, we can often accomplish tasks without understanding a lot of the language in the authentic materials associated with the task. One might argue, then, that it is not important to know all language in the material because completing the task is the goal. We believe, however, that in many settings, particularly foreign language settings, the students need to learn language and not simply complete a task.

One example of a non-authentic task is some type of information gap activity with certain types of materials. For example, a teacher can assign students different movie clips to watch for homework. Students then get into groups with other students who watched different parts of the movie to reconstruct it. This type of activity is often done with readings, but in either case, it does not reflect something we do in real life.

Another information gap activity is one in which students are each given sentences from a reading and then have to put the sentences in order. If students have to memorize the sentences, they are more likely to hold chunks of language from the authentic passage in their heads. If the readings are too difficult for students to remember full sentences, they can be given different passages to read and then come together to answer a common set of questions for which they have to pool information from the different sections of the readings. This can work well with short one-page mysteries or, in an academic language class, with research articles divided to reflect different sections.

With beginners, a natural activity like reading a newspaper or listening to the news will be too difficult without huge amounts of support. Therefore, students can use authentic texts in ways that require very little comprehension of the text. For example, even on the first day of a French or Spanish class, students can be given a text, such as a short story, in which they can simply circle all the cognates. The goal of this activity is not to understand the text but to alert students to how much they may already know about the target language. Students can return to the text for other controlled activities such as finding certain verb tenses. Eventually, they will begin to read for meaning and can do more meaning-based activities.

2. Use explicit instruction and form-focused activities for certain grammatical forms in the texts.

This suggestion is relatively straightforward and is based on the numerous studies that have shown positive effects for explicit instruction. There are, however, many ways to provide explicit instruction and many points in a lesson in which it can be done. For example, teachers can choose a text and then do a lesson on a grammatical structure that students will need to understand the text. In many cases, programs use structurally organized textbooks and so teachers will do the opposite, namely, find a text that includes the forms they want to teach. In either case, it can be helpful to include some instruction on the target form and then have the students use the text for a grammar-focused activity such as a cloze task in which certain structures are deleted. One question is whether this type of activity should be done before the students read for meaning or after. If the students can get the main idea without fully understanding the grammatical form to be taught, they can be asked to read the text for homework and then do a form-focused activity such as the cloze in class. Another approach is to take the first few paragraphs from a reading and have the students do the activity as a type of pre-reading exercise. A cloze activity forces the students to read closely, and then they will be better prepared to read the remainder of the text. The point is that not only is the activity not authentic, but it can be combined with explicit instruction on grammar.

Dictoglosses in which a certain forms appear several times can also be combined with explicit instruction before or after the students complete the dictogloss. Sometimes it may be helpful to have students struggle with the structure in the dictogloss so that they will be more primed to learn the new structure. On the other hand, if teachers sense their students will become too frustrated with the new structure, it can be explicitly taught ahead of time. In fact, the explicit instruction will draw the students' attention to the form and they will be more likely to notice it during the listening phase of the dictogloss.

3. Vary the modality of the task even if it differs from the modality of the authentic task.

As discussed (see also Myth 3), one point of the reading-while-listening activity is that reading can support the skill of listening, particularly if students have stronger reading skills. Conversely, in the case of a heritage learner, the student may have stronger listening skills and listening can support reading. The point is that teachers can vary and mix modalities even if they are not the modalities used by the students in the authentic task.

With regard to listening, listening to extended authentic texts can be difficult because students can lose track of the meaning and get frustrated. They can also be sidelined by only a few difficult vocabulary words or unknown proper nouns. Transcripts of authentic texts can be used for a wide variety of activities to help students listen to extended texts. Simply giving the students challenging sentences from the spoken text to analyze or paraphrase will help them focus on meaning while listening because they will have already decoded some of the more challenging language. Another option is to give them sentences from the listening text and ask them to try to predict the order. As the students listen, they can try to put the sentence in the correct order from the text. Again, the point is that the written sentences will provide support as they listen to the spoken text.

We want to emphasize again that writing is a way to draw learners' attention to language and give them a chance to try to solve production problems that they would not have time to work through in oral production. We gave examples of dictoglosses and a story continuation activity. Additional activities might involves writing summaries using specified vocabulary from the story or paraphrasing challenging sentences. Students can also be given stories or non-fiction texts with paragraphs missing and be asked to create their own paragraph that makes sense. The goal is not the writing itself but the close reading that is needed to complete the task.

4. Move beyond discussion activities at the advanced level.

With beginners, we often cannot use authentic tasks because they require a certain level of comprehension of a text that cannot be achieved early in language study. For advanced learners, the problem is different. They can fully understand a text and complete an authentic task, but the text may contain several words or structures that the students cannot use. We addressed this in Myth 5 when we talked about the fact that classroom discussions did not lead to language improvement (e.g., Pica, 2002, and Darhower, 2014). In our study of Spanish literature classes (Polio & Zyzik, 2009), we noted that despite the fact that students felt that their listening and reading skills were strong, their speaking and writing skills did not progress in their advanced literature courses. The activities in these courses generally involve reading, discussion, and writing about the texts. We argued that more controlled language-focused activities were needed to help students progress. Any of the activities discussed in this chapter could be used to supplement discussions of and writing about the text.

Another issue that may come up with advanced students is that they can produce comprehensible language in discussions or other authentic tasks but they still make grammatical errors that do not impede comprehension by others. One possible task for them is to ask them to record a group discussion or a narrative and then ask them to transcribe their own language (Lynch, 2007). As they do this, they are likely to notice problems in their speech and correct them. This activity could also be used as a follow up to role play with beginner or intermediate students.

Epilogue

After reading the preceding seven chapters, in which we argue for the merits of authentic texts, the reader may be under the impression that we rely exclusively on authentic texts in our own classrooms. This is not the case, and thus, one of the central issues we will address in the epilogue is the appropriate use of non-authentic or simplified texts. Furthermore, we want to contextualize some of the criticisms of authentic texts or text-based teaching more generally (see especially, Long, 2007, 2015). Next, we address the issue of finding a balance between authentic and non-authentic texts, which involves knowing the goals and needs of your learner population. We conclude with some of the longstanding challenges of using authentic texts and a call for further research that directly studies the use of authentic materials.

Simplified Texts and Extensive Reading

One of the most popular uses of simplified texts occurs in the context of extensive reading programs. Extensive reading refers to pleasure reading, which is characterized by reading large quantities of relatively easy material (see Day & Bamford, 1998, for additional design features of extensive reading programs). The goal of reading extensively is to achieve general comprehension and enjoyment rather than taking a comprehension quiz or doing an in-depth analysis of the text during class. Accordingly, extensive reading is often presented in opposition to intensive reading, which involves reading shorter texts at a more diffi-cult level, generally for the purpose of locating specific information in the text and/or focusing on the language therein.

Most teachers and researchers agree that extensive reading can be a positive addition to a language course, giving learners access to large amounts of comprehensible input in the target language. Empirical evidence in support of extensive reading is growing, showing benefits in terms of reading speed/fluency, reading proficiency, vocabulary acquisition, and affective variables such as confidence and motivation. A recent meta-analysis by Nakanishi (2015) suggests that the benefits of extensive reading are tangible, with the largest effect size for pre-test/post-test contrasts (i.e., the same group was tested before and after an extensive reading program). Nation (2015) enthusiastically endorses extensive reading as a vital component of the *meaning-focused input* strand of any language course and also as a contributor to fluency development.

Most extensive reading research has utilized simplified texts, that is, graded readers. The reason for this is simple: extensive reading requires, by definition, reading a lot. Naturally, reading in large quantities is contingent on the material being relatively easy or at the right level for the reader (what is 'at the right level' is not easy to determine but is contingent to some extent on the learner's current vocabulary knowledge). As far as quantity of reading, Nation (2015) maintains that the minimum amount should be one graded reader every two weeks. Uden, Schmitt, and Schmitt (2014) conducted a study in which their participants read one book per week, which they describe as a "comfortable pace" (p. 10) for the participants. Chang and Millet (2015) had their students read 20 graded readers over the course of 26 weeks, which is slightly less than one book per week. With the exception of advanced learners, it would be unrealistic to use authentic texts in a reading program that progresses at such a rapid pace. In other words, simplified texts allow for the implementation of extensive reading with learners of all proficiency levels, including beginners and intermediates.

To summarize, it seems that extensive reading and simplified texts are an optimal combination. If teachers wish to incorporate extensive reading into their curriculum, they should consider primarily graded readers, especially for beginners and intermediate-level learners. Despite the inherent value of authentic texts, it must be recognized that their vocabulary load is too high for most L2 learners if they are to engage in independent reading (i.e., without assistance, without consulting a dictionary, etc.). Nation (2006) estimates that a learner needs to know 8000-9000 word families in order to read authentic novels in English. Research also suggests that readers need to know about 98 percent of the words in a text in order to comprehend it (Schmitt, Jiang, & Grabe, 2011). In practice, this means that a learner with a limited vocabulary will be hampered by many unknown words in authentic texts, making reading laborious. Nation and Deweerdt (2001) summarized the problem this way:

> For learners of English with a vocabulary smaller than 2000 words, most unsimplified text is just too difficult and does not provide the conditions necessary for learning through meaning-focused input. (p. 62)

However, these authors also recognize that "struggling with difficult text" (p. 62) is valuable, but it falls under the rubric of *language-focused learning*. On this view, simplified texts and authentic texts serve different purposes in a language course. Simplified texts, designed to be easy reading that learners do independently, provide meaning-focused input. Authentic texts, which are difficult and thus require pedagogical support, serve as material for intensive reading in the language-focused strand of the course.

One reason we are in favor of using simplified texts for the purposes of extensive reading is that reading can become a component of language learning from the very early levels. In this way, you can design a curriculum in which all learners—including first-semester students—are reading in the target language. Beginners and intermediates are not deprived of reading because they are reading texts that are right for their level of proficiency. Furthermore, the sheer quantity of reading done in extensive reading programs exceeds the amount of reading that happens in traditional classrooms where students might read a few short passages from their textbook each week.

Although authentic texts can be used with beginners (see Myth 1), they are not generally used for extensive reading as described here. The study by Maxim (2002), in which first-year German students read a

142-page German romance novel, might seem to be an exception. Nevertheless, we note that Maxim's approach is actually more aligned with *intensive reading* because the students were reading collaboratively in-class, completing exercises based on a novel that "presented a challenge [to them]" (Maxim, 2002, p. 23), and reading one novel over the course of ten weeks. In other words, this is quite different from the standard application of extensive reading in which learners read copious amounts of material that is easy for them.

Since graded readers are such a good fit for extensive reading, why not continue with simplified readers forever? Moreover, will learners be able to make the transition to authentic texts if they've been exposed to a steady diet of graded readers? These are legitimate questions that are now beginning to receive scrutiny in the research. A fact about graded readers is that they culminate at a certain vocabulary range—usually at the 3,000-word level. If learners are going to learn mid-frequency vocabulary (i.e., beyond the 3,000-word level), authentic texts will play a pivotal role. Fortunately, research by Uden, Schmitt, and Schmitt (2014) suggests that motivated readers can make a smooth progression to authentic novels from the highest-level graded readers. Their participants were able to read the authentic novels without much decline in reading comprehension, reading speed, or satisfaction. Interestingly, there were mixed results in terms of enjoyment of the authentic novels, but this had to do with the content/themes of the books and not with the fact that they were authentic. Uden et al. defend the position that we have "the right not to finish a book" (Pennac, 2006, p. 145), which reminds us that some authentic material will be interesting and motivating for our learners—and some will not.

Responding to Criticisms of Text-Based Teaching

Long (2007, 2015) has argued convincingly in favor of structuring language curricula around tasks rather than texts. In his view of Task-Based Language Teaching (TBLT), functional language proficiency is achieved by engaging learners in tasks that are relevant to their communicative needs (e.g., following directions on a street map of Seoul, negotiating a police traffic stop, opening a bank account). This approach prizes learning by doing rather than studying language as an object. Given this orientation, it is not surprising that Long criticizes texts as a foundation for developing language courses and the way in which they are typically used in language classrooms. Long (2007) gives the example of a reading passage describing a chemistry experiment, which is arguably very different from actually doing a chemistry experiment oneself in a laboratory. For Long, "texts are frozen records or someone else's prior task accomplishment" (p. 120) and will do little to help learners perform a similar task in real life.

It is not our intent to dispute Long's arguments about the importance of doing tasks in order to develop the linguistic and pragmatic skills needed to function in the workplace, in the community, or in academic settings. However, it is important to understand that TBLT also involves texts (spoken and/or written) at certain points in the pedagogical sequence. Crucially, these texts are not "ends in themselves" (Long, 2007, p. 130), but only one step along the way to eventually performing the target task. In this context, Long acknowledges that exposing students to realistic samples of language is a thorny problem. If we want students to be able to schedule a doctor's appointment, open a bank account, or order dinner in a restaurant, then what kind of language samples should serve as input? Long (2015) discusses this issue at length, presenting, at first, two equally unsatisfactory solutions. On one hand, there is the traditional solution of simplified input, which he strongly rejects (see discussion of simplification in Myth 6). On the other hand, he critiques authentic texts for being too difficult for all but advanced learners; they present "too dense of a linguistic target" and can impede learning "by confronting learners with large amounts of unknown language [. . .] without compensatory devices to facilitate comprehension" (Long, 2007, p. 130). Long ultimately favors the inclusion of modified texts, specifically those that are elaborated rather than simplified.

For Long (2015), authenticity is "a fashionable attempt" (p. 249) to supplement or replace the simplified dialogues of most commercially produced language textbooks. Upon close inspection, it seems that Long's critique of authentic texts is embedded in a more general critique of text-based approaches. He disapproves of any approach in which texts are used to highlight the grammatical structures exemplified in them, which might reflect a covert or overt structural syllabus, and thus, is antithetical to TBLT. Even in content-based instruction, where learners read authentic texts about specific topics that are often aligned with their academic interests, Long (2007) believes that, "most text-based instruction is simply a variant of structurally based teaching at the sentence level" (p. 121). In other words, it is difficult to isolate the specific case against authentic texts from a more general rejection of text-based teaching.

We concur with Long (2007, 2015) in that simply exposing students to texts, be they authentic or non-authentic, is not enough. In fact, one of our goals in writing this book was to highlight the numerous activities that teachers can do in order to exploit authentic texts in terms of both content and language. For example, in Myth 4 we discussed the various activities that can be done to scaffold learning prior to working with authentic texts; in Myth 1 we presented options that are suitable for beginners, such as examining information in a table and comparing it to their personal lives (see Appendix A). Myth 5 presents ideas that target the development of speaking and writing skills. A common thread in our chapters is that authentic texts are just raw material, and opportunities for language development arise when we ask learners to go beyond the text in some way.

Although Long (2015) opposes the use of authentic texts with lower-proficiency learners, his sample tasks for advanced learners rely heavily on authentic texts. For example, learners are asked to conduct research and report on a complex political issue (e.g., tensions between the autonomous regions and Spain's central government). In order to carry out this task, learners view and read a variety of authentic texts, including TV news broadcasts, political speeches, and academic publications relevant to the topic (see the pedagogic tasks in his Table 9.11 on pages 293–294). Authentic texts figure prominently in the realization of the task, allowing students to delve into intellectually demanding content, fine-tune their language skills, and gain in-depth cultural knowledge about a particular region/country.

This last example leads us to an important point: authentic texts are vital in giving students an opportunity to interact with stimulating content. In our experience as teachers, many (but not all) L2 learners are interested in the social, cultural, or political issues affecting the country or region where the target language is spoken. This is where authentic texts come into play, especially those that reflect the personal stories, experiences, and opinions of real people from the target culture. A good example of this is given in Hertel and Harrington (2015), who describe the use of Spanish-language documentary films and present a syllabus for an entire course that centers on these (authentic) texts. Documentaries form the core of the advanced-level course, which covers issues such as immigration, globalization, and poverty. In contrast with other types of authentic texts, documentaries have the distinct advantage of exposing learners to unscripted speech. In addition, they often focus on controversial issues that are generally absent from textbooks. Crucially, Hertel and Harrington present a wide array of "task-oriented activities" (p. 554) that can be done to engage students with the content and the language of the documentaries. Clearly, students are doing much more than just watching the films and talking about them in class. For example, students write a diary entry from the point of view of a person interviewed in the film, analyze regional (or social) dialect features of the characters, and participate in a debate on one of the social issues explored in the documentary.

In sum, our perspective is one in which texts and tasks are not mutually exclusive. Authentic texts, which motivate and engage learners with relevant and stimulating content, can be used as the basis for a number of tasks to promote language acquisition.

Finding a Balance between Authentic and Non-Authentic Texts

There is no prescribed formula for finding this balance, but we will offer a few ideas for consideration. On a macro-level (i.e., when considering the entire curriculum for a foreign language program and articulation between the levels), we would expect the proportion of authentic texts to increase with advancement in proficiency. In other words, a first-semester course might include a relatively small number of authentic texts, which are used to supplement a textbook designed for L2 learners. As learners make progress and achieve gains in proficiency, they would be expected to process larger amounts of authentic text. At the more advanced level, the entire course could be based on authentic texts, as is the norm in content-based instruction. A recent example of this is described in Bartlett and Manyé (2015), who designed a course on contemporary Spain around a television series as the primary text. Likewise in courses that fall under the rubric of languages for specific purposes (LSP) such Medical Spanish, we might expect a relatively high proportion of authentic texts.

Another fundamental consideration is the type of learner we are teaching. In particular, for heritage speakers, we would argue that authentic texts should be used (almost) exclusively. It is well know that heritage language learners (HLLs) are different from foreign language learners in terms of the linguistic and cultural knowledge they bring to the classroom. Using simplified materials designed for L2 learners with HLLs is likely to be ineffective, and in the worst case, harmful. Helmer (2014) describes a Spanish class for HLLs at the high-school level in which students engaged in "performance strikes," which were evident in disruptive behavior and an overall lack of engagement with Spanish class. At the root of the problem was the teacher's use of a textbook designed for L2 learners and episodes of a simplified *telenovela* (soap-opera) that accompanied the textbook. The HLLs rejected the *telenovela* for its inauthenticity, an expected reaction considering that many of them had viewed authentic *telenovelas* in their households. Helmer concludes that, "the teacher's choice to use foreign language materials likely discredited the students' linguistic competence and seemingly denied their social identities as target-language insiders" (p. 194).

Another context where authentic texts predominate or are used exclusively are content-based curricula. Consider a content-based course such as "Environment and Sustainability in Latin America" taught in Spanish. The primary concern when choosing instructional materials for such a course will be content relevance. The teacher will want to teach the content in a way that presents accurate information and exposes students to various viewpoints. In institutions that teach courses such as this, the use of authentic texts is paramount. A well-known example of such a program is the Middlebury Institute of International Studies (MIIS), which offers Master's degrees in diverse fields with an international focus. Professional working proficiency in the target language is a central component of these programs and students take courses such as "Current issues in non-proliferation," "Comparative environmental policies," and "International gender issues." Some courses are taught by a combination of content specialists and language faculty (see Howard & Matsuo, 2014 for details). Since these graduate students are learning the language in order to use it in professional settings that require country-specific knowledge, it makes sense to use authentic texts exclusively. However, as noted by Howard and Matsuo, developing such courses was a time-consuming process, a point that we return to later when addressing the longstanding challenges of authentic texts.

Yet another type of context, arguably very different from the graduate program at MIIS, is one for adult immigrants studying ESL. These learners need to navigate daily interactions in the real world, including survival-type situations such a opening a bank account or filling out forms at the local elementary school. In this context, Roberts and Cooke (2009) argue that authentic texts are critically important precisely because of the complex nature of these institutional interactions. Roberts and Cooke explain that simplified materials do not prepare immigrants for interaction in the real world and, in some sense, do them a disservice by presenting "an idealised interactional world in which people use the same variety of standard English, everyone co-operates, . . . and all participants are equally legitimate speakers" (p. 624). They show this by examining the interactional features of simplified materials in two contexts (medical consultation and job interview) and comparing them to real-life scenarios in the same contexts. Roberts and Cooke conclude that the simplified materials are indeed oversimplified and thus distort or "flatten out" (p. 639) interactional complexity. Although Roberts and Cooke seem to propose the exclusive use of authentic texts with immigrant populations, we see the opportunity for a balanced approach. Authentic texts based on corpora could be used for the purposes of teaching features of spoken interaction (as Roberts & Cooke suggest), but simplified texts such as graded readers could be used to promote reading and build vocabulary. Ultimately, such decisions would depend on the profile of the learners and the goals of the curriculum.

Challenges of Using Authentic Materials

Some of the challenges of using authentic materials have already been alluded to throughout this book. There are non-trivial issues surrounding access to authentic, unscripted interactions such as doctor-patient conversations. Roberts and Cooke (2009) explain that, "collecting naturally occurring real-life data is time-consuming and expensive and access to sites to record events such as job interviews and medical consultations is difficult to gain" (p. 631). A similar issue is confronted by Long (2015) with the example of negotiating a police traffic stop. It seems that some of the most interesting types of interactions we would want to study in a language class are precisely the ones that are protected by confidentiality or are otherwise private. Other types of unscripted spoken language, such as academic lectures, should be easier to obtain. Wagner (2014) recommends that teachers record routine conversations or phone calls with family and friends (with the participants' permission) to be later used in the classroom.

Another challenge, all too familiar to language teachers, is that it is time-consuming to search for, compile, and organize authentic texts. In some contexts, courses that rely heavily on authentic texts are developed by a team of faculty rather than by an individual teacher (cf. Howard & Matsuo, 2014). Some types of authentic texts are easily reused and thus worth the effort in the initial round of course preparation (e.g., a short story or poem). The problem is especially acute if the content is related to current events. Consider, for example, a course on Latin American politics (or a thematic unit on this topic within a more general course). Since political events are constantly unfolding, if the materials are not current they become less relevant and thus less useful. On the other hand, this is one of the greatest rewards of working with authentic texts: students perceive the relevance of timely materials that speak to events happening outside of the classroom.

The use of authentic reading materials in Chinese and Japanese can provide additional challenges because of the possibility of learners not knowing enough characters to help them understand the texts. In alphabetic languages, learners can at least look up words and use phonological cues, whereas looking up Chinese and Japanese characters is very time consuming and phonological cues are not terribly helpful. Even after a year of study, students may have great difficulty reading a newspaper article. One way to work with authentic materials in beginning Chinese and Japanese classes is to use them simply for character recognition activities. Using the same couple of texts, students can return to them periodically to see which characters they know until they can comprehend portions of the texts. We want to point out also that Chinese movies and television shows generally include Chinese character captions. These might be useful in helping learners make the connections between oral language and characters. Unfortunately, most of the existing research on captions focuses on helping listening skills. Vanderplank (2010), in his review of research on video and television viewing reported on only one empirical study that examined the effect of captions on literacy (Kothari, Pandey, & Chudgar, 2004, as cited in Vanderplank). The study found a positive effect on reading in English, but it was not an experimental study and participants self-selected into the viewing and non-viewing groups. Thus, the effect of captions on literacy is an area wide open for further research.

Finally, we have to point out the curricular realities of incorporating authentic materials in large language programs with multiple sections of the same course. Often, instructors have to follow the same syllabus with the same textbook and students take common exams. The textbook may not include many authentic texts, but it makes for a uniform curriculum. Instructors may want to supplement the textbook with authentic materials but they cannot do so because of time constraints related to covering the required material. One solution is for instructors to each develop a lesson or lessons using authentic materials that are then shared; this also reduces the instructors' workload. Another option is to have instructors cover less of the textbook that is used for the common exam. Each instructor can then assess their own students on lessons using the authentic materials.

Future Research on Authentic Materials

Despite the fact that there is a lot of research supporting the use of authentic materials, we have stated several times throughout this book that there is little empirical research comparing the use of authentic versus non-authentic materials. We noted in the introduction that studies such as Gilmore (2011), which compared classes using authentic and non-authentic materials, are not common. His ambitious quasi-experimental study compared EFL classes in Japan that used authentic and non-authentic materials for ten months. He found the authentic group outperformed the non-authentic group on eight out of thirteen measures, and on no measures did the experimental group do better. But these types of studies are challenging to do because it is difficult to keep the conditions similar in two groups over an extended period of time. In fact, sometimes the experimental group will do better simply because of the novelty of the treatment. Nevertheless, Gilmore's study was a useful step in showing that one can build a curriculum using authentic materials and that students will still do as well or better on various proficiency measures. His study would be useful to conceptually replicate in other foreign language settings.

Appendix A
Myth 1 Activity

About this authentic text: This text comes from a press release published in June 2010 (http://www.ine.es/prensa/np606.pdf) that summarizes a national survey on how Spaniards use their time. The portion of the document that we include here is a summary table that shows the results by activity (e.g., *trabajo remunerado* "paid work") and by gender (*varones* "men" and *mujeres* "women"). The complete text includes more details, including what types of activities are included in each category. For example, the category *cuidados personales* "personal care" includes time spent sleeping and having meals.

Text source: Instituto Nacional de Estadísticas (Spanish Statistical Office) http://www.ine.es)

Porcentaje de personas que realizan la actividad en el transcurso del día y duración media diaria dedicada a la actividad por dichas personas. 2009-2010

Actividades Principales	Total personas		Varones		Mujeres	
	% de personas	Duración media diaria	% de personas	Duración media diaria	% de personas	Duración media diaria
0 Cuidados personales	100,0	11:32	100,0	11:35	100,0	11:29
1 Trabajo remunerado	33,5	7:20	38,6	7:54	28,6	6:35
2 Estudios	14,8	5:18	14,4	5:27	15,1	5:09
3 Hogar y familia	83,5	3:34	74,4	2:28	92,2	4:25
4 Trabajo voluntario y reuniones	11,8	1:50	9,1	2:01	14,4	1:43
5 Vida social y diversión	57,0	1:43	56,0	1:49	58,1	1:38
6 Deportes y actividades al aire libre	38,4	1:46	41,8	1:57	35,1	1:33
7 Aficiones e informática	29,7	1:52	36,0	2:02	23,6	1:37
8 Medios de comunicación	88,4	3:00	87,7	3:08	89,0	2:51
9 Trayectos y tiempo no especificado	84,6	1:23	87,4	1:25	82,0	1:21

We see this text as a rich source of information that can be exploited in numerous ways with beginners, especially since most first-year classes devote a lot of time to talking about daily activities and routines. The teacher will need to guide the students in understanding the text by explaining any unknown vocabulary, noting the use of commas (not periods) in numerals, and the kind of information that is presented (percentages, duration).

Possible teaching options:

1. Ask students to compare the data in the table with their own use of time. Before showing students the text, give them a list of the 10 categories (*cuidados personales, estudios, hogar y familia,* etc.) and explain any unknown vocabulary. Then, ask them to estimate how much time they spend on each activity in a typical day. They can do this individually and then work in groups to compare their habits. The last step would be to compare their responses to the data from Spain, noting similarities and differences. With beginners, it is important to give them a very specific task such as "list two differences and two similarities."

2. Use the text as a basis for cross-cultural comparison between Spaniards' use of time and that of the local culture. One way to do this is to give students an incomplete version of the text, removing the categories in the left-hand column (e.g., *cuidados personales, estudios, hogar y familia*). Project the categories on the board and have students fill in the table based on their perceptions of how Spaniards spend their time. The next step would be to compare their version of the table with the original, noting any discrepancies. Is there anything about Spaniards' use of time that surprises them? Is it very different from the habits of Americans?

3. Use the text as a springboard for discussion about gender roles; it may be more appropriate for more advanced beginners or intermediate learners. Before looking at the text, ask students to guess if men or women spend more time doing the activities in the 10 categories. To facilitate this, the teacher can give them a worksheet to fill out. They can do this in groups, with some discussion as a whole class. Finally, they should compare their opinions with the information in the text, noting any discrepancies between what they believed to be true and what the data indicates. We note that this type of activity is perfectly compatible with a language focus on comparative structures (e.g., *más que* "more than," *menos que* "less than").

Appendix B
Myth 2 Activity

About this authentic text: *Radio Ambulante* is a Spanish-language podcast that presents thought provoking human-interest stories on a variety of topics related to Latin America. The podcasts are authentic (learners are not the intended audience), but they can be incorporated into the classroom for a variety of purposes. A noteworthy feature of these podcasts is that they contain segments of unscripted speech and represent different dialects of Spanish. In 2014, Radio Ambulante was awarded the Gabriel García Márquez Prize for Innovation in Journalism, the most prestigious journalism honor in Latin America. This podcast is now part of National Public Radio (NPR). For this appendix we have chosen an episode entitled *Los huérfanos* [The orphans], which tells the incredible story of two Nigerian children traveling through Mexico in a precarious situation. Although it can be used as the basis for a listening comprehension activity (with no focus on grammar), we present some ideas for using this text to teach direct and indirect object pronouns. The episode is 17 minutes long, so depending on available class time, some portions of this pedagogical sequence could be assigned as homework.

Text: Source: Radio Ambulante (http://radioambulante.org)
http://radioambulante.org/audio/los-huerfanos

Possible teaching sequence:

1. Listen to the podcast for meaning first. Students must listen to the text in order to engage with the meaning, that is, understand what the story is about. As with any authentic text, decide what kind of pre-listening is needed, depending on the level of the students. The pre-listening might take the form of topic

preparation and/or pre-teaching some key vocabulary words, especially those specific to this variety of Spanish (e.g., *chamarra* ["coat"]). Listen to the first five minutes of the podcast in class and then ask the students to predict what will happen to the children.

2. Conduct comprehension checks. We are still in the first phase, listening for meaning. Check students' understanding of the story. Since this is a relatively long text (17 minutes), check comprehension after shorter segments. For example, after the first three minutes teachers might ask: *What is odd about the two children traveling on the bus? What kind of person is Jazmín?* After five minutes, teachers might ask: *What kind of person is Tanisha, the woman accompanying the children? Do you think she is their mother?*

3. A grammar focus can be achieved in various ways. Now that students have established the meaning of the story, they can make new form-meaning connections (or consolidate them).

    A. Working with the transcript of the podcast (available on the Radio Ambulante website), select a portion of the podcast that contains direct and/or indirect object pronouns. Make copies of the transcript for students and number the segments that you will focus on. Ask students to identify the referents of the pronouns. For example, after Tanisha leaves for the United States and Jasmín exclaims, ". . . *que no los haya dejado abandonados*" [I hope she hasn't abandoned them], ask students who is *los* referring to? Identifying the referent of the pronoun is facilitated by the students' comprehension of the story.

    B. Create a dictation activity based on the podcast. Select a segment and delete certain verbs (including the direct or indirect object pronouns that accompany them). Read the text orally and ask students to fill in the missing words or phrases they hear. As they compare their work with the original, make sure they have the right form of the pronoun (direct/indirect, singular/plural, masculine/feminine).

C. Do a dictogloss activity with portions of this text. Choose a segment that is an appropriate length (four to six sentences in length). As students reconstruct the text and later compare it with the original, make sure to focus their attention on the pronouns and their placement.

D. For a more advanced class, ask students to underline or circle all the direct and indirect object pronouns in the transcript. Then ask them to make two columns with all the verbs that appear with indirect objects (e.g., *ofrecer* ["offer"], *prestar* ["lend"]) in one column and all the verbs that appear with direct objects (e.g., *conocer* ["to know"], *abandonar* ["abandon"]) in the second column. Afterward, lead them to reflect on what these verbs have in common; students should notice that the majority of the indirect objects appear with verbs that take three arguments. Also, they will note that indirect objects are often reduplicated (e.g., *yo decidí prestarle la chamarra al niño* ["I decided to lend the coat to the child"]). In contrast, direct objects are not reduplicated.

E. Extension activity: Ask students to write a brief news report on the case of the Nigerian children. They have to summarize the facts of the story according to what they heard in the podcast. Later, they can compare their news story to one of the published reports in the Mexican press (see for example, http://www.jornada.unam.mx/ultimas).

Appendix C
Myth 3 Activity

About this authentic text: The examples here come from the book, *The Hunger Games*. Novel-length young adult literature can be used effectively in language classes because while the language is often not too difficult, the themes can be interesting for adult learners. Furthermore, if accompanying movies are available, these can be used along with the novels to teach listening skills. *The Hunger Games* can be read on a variety of levels, and instructors can include themes related to the role of the government, war, and freedom. We encourage you to seek out young adult literature in other target languages.

Text source: *The Hunger Games* by Suzane Collins.

Possible teaching sequence:

What you do with the text will vary according to the students' levels and how much time you have to spend with the text. This sequence could be done over a couple of weeks or extended throughout a semester. The goal of these activities is both to show students that they can understand (and hopefully enjoy) a longer text as well to exploit the text for language-focused activities. The activities can be used with any novel.

1. Include some type of schema activation or schema building activity.

    A. If many of the students are familiar with the plot, ask them to get into groups and collaboratively write a plot summary. Then, reconvene the class and reconstruct the plot on the board or projector. As you do this, include important vocabulary in your reconstruction and underline the words.

B. If students are not familiar with the plot, create an internet scavenger hunt in which they have to answer a series of questions about the novel by searching online (e.g., *How many books are in the series? What is the name of the female protagonist?*). Use these as a basis for a class discussion.

2. For each chapter, include both a top-down activity focused on meaning and a bottom-up activity focused on language.

   A. A top-down activity might have the students read the first chapter and make a list of all the characters as well as what they know about each character.

   B. A bottom-up activity might include a grammar or vocabulary cloze test such as this example:

Fill in the blanks with a form of the appropriate phrasal verb: *to split open, to knock back, to take in, to break off, to lean back.*

When my stomach feels like it's about to _____, I _____ and _____ my breakfast companions. Peeta is still eating, _____ bits of roll and dipping them in hot chocolate. Haymitch hasn't paid much attention to his platter, but he's _____ a glass of red juice that he keeps thinning with a clear liquid from a bottle. Judging by the fumes, it's some kind of spirit. I don't know Haymitch, but I've seen him often enough in the Hobe, tossing handfuls of money on the counter of the women who sell white liquor. He'll be incoherent by the time we reach the Capitol.

---

3. Create exercises from earlier chapters so that students have to go back and reread. These activities can be more challenging because students should have a better idea of the meaning and context of the text. The paragraph shown is very challenging because of the descriptive language. The goal is get the students to guess possible words and to focus on language that they might have missed while trying to understand the story. Note that no word bank is given, so the activity is quite difficult.

When I passed the _____, the smell of fresh bread was so overwhelming I felt _____. The ovens were in the back, and a golden _____ spilled out the open kitchen door. I stood mesmerized by the heat and the _____ scent until the rain interfered, running its _____ fingers down my back, forcing me back to life. I lifted the lid to the baker's trash bin and found it spotlessly, heartlessly _____ .

---

4. End with some type of project. Some examples include:

   A. Take a chapter and ask students to write a movie scene. They can then watch the scene from the movie and compare it with what they wrote.
   B. Ask students to write something like a book club reading guide for the book.
   C. Ask students to interview people who have read the book. They can write a summary of people's opinions of the book.

Appendix D
Myth 4 Activity

About this authentic text: TED (Technology, Entertainment, Design) talks are available free of cost online at www.ted.com. Some talks come with lessons (www.ted.com/watch/ted-ed) that include multiple choice and discussion questions as well as additional resources. The talks are in English, and are often used in ESL classes. Some talks have subtitles in other languages, but they are not useful for teaching languages other than English. If you are looking for talks in other languages, try TEDx, which organizes independent talks in a variety of languages (http://tedxtalks.ted.com/pages/languageplaylists). TED talks are generally educational, interesting, and engaging. Many ESL teachers like to use them because they in some ways resemble academic lectures but they are accessible to a wide audience.

Text source: www.ted.com/talks/amy_cuddy_your_body_language_shapes_who_you_are/transcript?language+en (Includes both audio passages and transcripts.)

This activity focuses on both vocabulary and grammar by teaching students noun-noun compounds in English. There is likely some new vocabulary as well as some familiar compounds (e.g., *car accident*). In addition, many of these can be considered chunks or common collocations (e.g., *animal kingdom, business school*).

Possible teaching sequence:

1. The teacher explains that a noun can be modified with an adjective such as in the expression *terrible accident* or *famous school*, but that speakers can also use nouns to modify other nouns as in *car accident* or *business school*. The students are asked to look at noun-noun combinations from a talk that they will listen to.

147

The students should first look at the two lists (shown) and circle any words that they don't understand at all (e.g., *gubernatorial, rehab*). (Words in parentheses are adjectives).

body	hierarchies
physician-patient	males
(gubernatorial) race	condition
power	board
animal	non-verbals
power	rehab ward
MBA	hormone
business	situations
gender	interview
primate	people
stress	school
high-power pose	grade gap
school	outcomes
(social) threat	dynamics
job	language
car	kingdom
head injury	accident
high-power alpha	interactions
low-power	classrooms

2. Then ask students to match the words in the two columns to make plausible noun-noun combinations. The goal here is not to get all the right answers but to decide which might be possible. The teacher will lead a review of which combinations are possible and which are likely (see answers next page).

3. Give the students a second, clean handout with the two lists. While the video is playing for the first time, the students listen for the matches. During the second listening, they focus on the content. (Alternatively, the students can listen first for the general ideas, and then do the matching activity.)

5. Give students the sentences from the transcript with blanks and then ask them to fill in the blanks with one of the combinations. For example: *And those judgments can predict really _____ like who we hire or promote or who we ask out on a date.* After completing this activity, the students can listen to the video again.

Answers: Combinations found in the text.

body language	stress hormone
physician-patient interactions	high-power pose condition
(gubernatorial) race outcomes	school board
power dynamics	(social) threat situations
animal kingdom	job interview
power non-verbals	car accident
MBA classrooms	head injury rehab ward
business school	high-power alpha males
gender grade gap	low-power people
primate hierarchies	meaningful life outcomes

Appendix E
Myth 5 Activity

About this authentic text: This text comes from a German sports news website. It was chosen because it conveys cultural information about the importance of soccer in Germany, but also because women's soccer has become increasingly visible in the U.S., so students are likely to be familiar with the topic.

Text source: www.kicker.de/news/fussball/frauen/startseite/629358/artikel_mittag_mit-uns-ist-zu-rechnen.html

Mittag: "**Mit uns ist zu rechnen**"

Eitel Sonnenschein im Lager der deutschen Frauen-Nationalmannschaft: Das 4:1 im **WM-Achtelfinale** gegen Schweden war das erhoffte Ausrufezeichen, nach einer Vorrunde, die trotz des Gruppensieges nicht das wahre Leistungsvermögen der DFB-Frauen offenbarte. Die Partie am Samstagabend im Lansdowne Stadium in Ottawa hat indes die Titelambitionen **der Elf von Trainerin Silvia Neid** deutlich unterstrichen. Entsprechend gelöst präsentierte sich die Bundestrainerin.

"Ein sehr wichtiges Spiel, vielleicht ein **Schlüsselspiel**, weil wir bei dieser WM noch nicht so viele hatten von dieser Qualität." Die Einordnung, die Neid nach dem deutlichen und auch **hochverdienten Erfolg** gegen die Skandinavierinnen vornahm, zeigte die ganze Erleichterung über den erhofften "**Aha-Effekt**".

"Wir haben gezeigt: **Mit uns ist zu rechnen**", meinte dann auch Anja Mittag, die mit ihrem fünften Turniertor **in der 24. Minute** die DFB-Elf **in Führung** und damit ins Rollen **brachte**. **Mittag und Co.** waren nicht mehr aufzuhalten, die Schwedinnen um Stürmerstar Lotta Schelin konnten weder das deutsche Angriffsspiel entscheidend

150

unterbinden, noch für großartig **Gefahr vor dem Gehäuse** von Nadine Angerer sorgen.

Am Ende stand ein 4:1, das Celia Sasic mit zwei Toren und Dzsenifer Marozsan abrundeten. Vor allen Mittag und Sasic, die ebenfalls **fünf Tore auf dem Konto hat**, waren nicht zu bremsen. "**Wir ergänzen uns** sehr gut, ich gehe mehr in die Tiefe, Anja arbeitet super vor der Kette," ließ Sasic wissen. "Wir kennen uns schon ewig, <u>unser Spiel ist</u> daher <u>**gut abgestimmt**</u>. Dass **es für uns beide so gut läuft**, ist natürlich cool," meinte Mittag. Auch am Freitag, wenn es für die DFB-Frauen im Viertelfinale gegen Frankreich oder Südkorea weitergeht, kommt es auf das Duo an.

Possible teaching options:

Dictoglosses can be done in a variety of ways, but the goal is to get students to produce written language beyond what they could normally produce on their own. Note that it's possible to use an oral text as well, but because the activity is written, it is arguably better to use a written text that is related to something that the students might have to write in real life or that contains language similar to what students might have to write in real life. Teachers can choose a text related to the topic being covered. It's possible to choose texts related to specific vocabulary and grammar points as well, but authentic texts with specific grammar structures can be difficult to find.

A standard dictogloss is done by having the students listen to a text once to understand the overall meaning. The passage is then read two more times with the students taking notes. It should be read faster than a standard dictation so that students cannot write down every word. Students then try to reconstruct the passage as close to the original as possible; they should not try to summarize. The reconstruction is usually done in pairs because students will often talk about the language from the text and can share information with each other. The students then compare their passages to the original. The teacher can discuss how the students' reconstructions differ from the original.

A dictogloss can be done as a pre- or post-reading activity. If a text is difficult, it is probably better to do the activity after the students have read the material from which the excerpt is taken. If the material is not too difficult, excerpts from the beginning of the material can be used and serve as a pre-reading activity.

One variation is to provide students ahead of time with a list of chunks or phrases from the text. The purpose here is draw students' attention to these chunks and to get the students to then use them productively. In the German text, the chunks are highlighted in bold. (Chunks separated by other words are underlined.) The teacher gives students a handout with the chunks listed. After going over the phrases, the students complete the dictogloss while looking at the phrases.

Dictoglosses get students to use new language, but if you prefer a writing activity in which students are creating texts as opposed to reconstructing texts, you can do a similar activity in which students write a summary by following a different procedure.

Students are given the passage to read for homework and told that they need to understand it well and to look up any new words that they don't know.

In class, give students a list of words and proper nouns that are essential to writing a summary of the passage. For example: *die Frauen-Nationalmannschaft, das WM-Achtelfinale, Silvia Neid, das Schlüsselspiel, Anja Mittag, das Duo.* The students then write a summary using the given words without looking at the passage.

Appendix F
Myth 6 Activity

About this authentic text: This text comes from a memoir, *Incidents in an Educational Life* (2009, University of Michigan Press) written by John Swales, one of the authors cited in this book. In his book, Swales provides a variety of stories about his education, from his boyhood in England to events in his professional life as a scholar and researcher.

We chose this text because it addresses a topic, education, that might be discussed in a language class. It is written in a somewhat informal style and includes some colloquial language (e.g., *ripe old age*) as well as academic language (e.g., *prescient*) and cultural references to boarding school in England. It is likely a challenging passage to understand, but if were simplified or summarized, the power of the story that Swales is telling might be lost. The lesson is structured in a way that gets students to infer meaning based on the language used.

> When I had reached the ripe old age of nine or so, my parents decided that it was time for me to endure the rigors of boarding school. They probably felt that the school I had been attending was lacking somewhat in sanitation, nutrition, and the like, so they sent me to a school on the south coast of England. This school was run by two brothers, both of whom had been majors in the army, and they ran the school—perhaps in consequence—with great discipline as represented by a huge number of arcane rules. For one example, there were painted lines on many of the floors, and only third-years could cross red lines, and fourth-year blue lines, while first-years like me could hardly cross any lines at all! Worse, I was placed in the bottom class because I was new, even though I was older than most of the others in it. One of these majors took us for

geography, and one day asked us what kinds of power there were. I answered something like "wind power, water power, steam power, hydro-electric power, internal combustion power." I would like to think I would have added "nuclear power," although that might have been a bit prescient because I don't think the first nuclear power station in Britain was yet in operation. But I could see that the major, far from being pleased with my impressive answer, hated me for it. (p. 4–5)

Possible teaching sequence:

1. Ask students to skim the passage, turn it over, and try to answer the following questions in pairs.

    A. Who do you think the author is and how do you know?
    - i. Is the author male or female?
    - ii. What is the author's nationality?
    - iii. In what decade do you think this story took place?
    - iv. What kind of student do you think he or she was?

2. Ask students to reread the text and then decide if they want to modify their answers. Ask them why the teacher was not happy with the student's answer.

3. Ask the students to look at the text and underline any words or phrase they don't know. In groups, they can discuss the words they don't know without looking them up. After they do this, explain the words to the class.

4. A follow-up activity could include asking students to write a paragraph of a memorable experience that they had with a teacher.

Appendix G
Myth 7 Activity

About this authentic text: This text is the first paragraph of Albert Camus's novel *L'Etranger* ("The Stranger"). This famous novel is often used in French classes because the language is not difficult yet the themes are complex. The first two sentences alone are simple yet can elicit a lot of discussion. (Mother/mom died today. Or maybe yesterday, I don't know.)

> Aujourd'hui, maman est morte. Ou peut-être hier, je ne sais pas. J'ai reçu un télégramme de l'asile : « Mère décédée. Enterrement demain. Sentiments distingués. » Cela ne veut rien dire. C'était peut-être hier. L'asile de vieillards est à Marengo, à quatre-vingts kilomètres d'Alger. Je prendrai l'autobus 5 à deux heures et j'arriverai dans l'après-midi. Ainsi, je pourrai veiller et je rentrerai demain soir. J'ai demandé deux jours de congé à mon patron et il ne pouvait pas me les refuser avec une excuse pareille.

Chapter 1 of the novel can be found here: http://lettres.ac-orleans-tours.fr/fileadmin/user_upload/lettres/EAF_Doublants/Etranger/Etranger_incipit.pdf)

Possible teaching options:

This activity is non-authentic and does not reflect something that students would do with language in real life. The point of the activity is for students to focus on chunks of language and to focus on grammatical structures or words as they try to remember the sentence well enough to write it down. Teachers can use a complete short text, the first paragraph of a longer text that will be used later in class, or a self-contained excerpt. The excerpt is from the first paragraph of a novel and is not difficult, so it can be used before students have read the text. For more difficult passages that students may have skimmed over, such descriptive paragraphs, you can choose a passage that students have already read for homework. This activity will get them to read the passage more carefully.

1. The teacher places a list of out-of-order sentences on the board (or in a large class, several copies can be placed around the room) far enough so that students cannot read the sentences from their seats. For example:

   A. *J'ai demandé deux jours de congé à mon patron et il ne pouvait pas me les refuser avec une excuse pareille.*
   B. *Je prendrai l'autobus 5 à deux heures et j'arriverai dans l'après-midi.*
   C. *Aujourd'hui, maman est morte.*
   D. *Cela ne veut rien dire.*
   E. *L'asile de vieillards est à Marengo, à quatre-vingts kilomètres d'Alger.*
   F. *Ainsi, je pourrai veiller et je rentrerai demain soir.*
   G. *Ou peut-être hier, je ne sais pas.*
   H. *C'était peut-être hier.*
   I. *J'ai reçu un télégramme de l'asile : « Mère décédée. Enterrement demain. Sentiments distingués. »*

2. The students must go to the board, read a sentence, return to their seats, and write it down. They will do this until all the sentences have been written.

3. Once the students have written all of the sentences, they must order the sentences to make a coherent passage.

References

Abrams, Z. I. (2014). Using film to provide a context for teaching L2 pragmatics. *System*, *46*, 55–64.

Adair-Hauck, B., & Donato, R. (2002). The PACE model: A story-based approach to meaning and form for standards-based language learning. *The French Review*, *76*(2), 265–276.

Allen, D. (2009). A study of the role of relative clauses in the simplification of news texts for learners of English. *System*, *37*(4), 585–599.

Allen, E. D., Bernhardt, E. B., Berry, M. T., & Demel, M. (1988). Comprehension and text genre: An analysis of secondary school foreign language readers. *The Modern Language Journal*, *72*(2), 163–172.

Allen, H. W., & Paesani, K. (2010). Exploring the feasibility of a pedagogy of multiliteracies in introductory foreign language courses. *L2 Journal*, *2*, 119–142.

Alptekin, C. (2006). Cultural familiarity in inferential and literal comprehension in L2 reading. *System*, *34*(4), 494–508.

Alptekin, C. (2008, May). Multicompetence revisited: From EFL to ELF. Plenary speech presented at the 5th ELT Research Conference—Bridging the gap between theory and practice in ELT. Çanakkale Onsekiz Mart University, Turkey.

Alptekin, C., & Erçetin, G. (2011). Effects of working memory capacity and content familiarity on literal and inferential comprehension in L2 reading. *TESOL Quarterly*, *45*(2), 235–266.

Alvstad, C., & Castro, A. (2009). Conceptions of literature in university language courses. *The Modern Language Journal*, *93*(2), 170–184.

Aufderhaar. C. R. (2004). The influence of using discourse analysis techniques on the filtered speech of authentic audio text to improve pronunciation (Unpublished dissertation). University of Cincinnati.

Barbieri, F. (2015). Involvement in university classroom discourse: Register variation and Interactivity. *Applied Linguistics, 36*, 151–173.

Barbieri, F., & Eckhardt, S. E. (2007). Applying corpus-based findings to form-focused instruction: The case of reported speech. *Language Teaching Research, 11*(3), 319–346.

Barrette, C. M., Paesani, K., & Vinall, K. (2010). Toward an integrated curriculum: Maximizing the use of target language literature. *Foreign Language Annals, 43*(2), 216–230.

Bartlett, L., & Manyé, L. (2015). Television as Textbook: Cuéntame cómo pasó in the Spanish (Literature) Classroom. *Hispania, 98*(3), 511–512.

Benavides, C. (2015). Using a corpus in a 300-level Spanish grammar course. *Foreign Language Annals, 48*(2), 218–235.

Bernhardt, E. B. (2002). Research into the teaching of literature in a second language: What it says and how to communicate it to graduate students. In V. Scott & H. Tucker (Eds.), *Second language acquisition and the literature classroom: Fostering dialogues* (pp. 195–211). Boston: Heinle.

Bernhardt, E. B. (2011). *Understanding advanced second language reading.* New York: Routledge.

Biber, D., Johansson, S., Leech, G., Conrad, S., & Finegan, E. (1999). *Longman grammar of spoken and written English.* Harlow, U.K.: Longman.

Bloch, J. (2009). The design of an online concordancing program for teaching about reporting verbs. *Language Learning & Technology, 13*(1), 59–78.

Boulton, A. (2010). Data-driven learning: Taking the computer out of the equation. *Language Learning, 60*(3), 534–572.

Boxer, D., & Pickering, L. (1995). Problems in the presentation of speech acts in ELT materials: The case of complaints. *ELT Journal, 49*(1), 44–58.

Brantmeier, C. (2003). Does gender make a difference? Passage content and comprehension in second language reading. *Reading in a Foreign Language, 15*(1), 1–27.

Bridges, E. (2009). Bridging the gap: A literacy-oriented approach to teaching the graphic novel der erste Frühling. *Die Unterrichtspraxis/Teaching German, 42*(2), 152–161.

Brinton, D., Snow, M. A., & Wesche, M. (1989). *Content-based second language instruction*. New York: Newbury House.

Brown, R., Waring, R., & Donkaewbua, S. (2008). Incidental vocabulary acquisition from reading, reading-while-listening, and listening to stories. *Reading in a Foreign Language, 20*(2), 136–163.

Bueno, K. A. (2009). Got film? Is it a readily accessible window to the target language and culture for your students? *Foreign Language Annals, 42*(2), 318–339.

Bunch, G. C., Walqui, A., & Pearson, P. D. (2014). Complex text and new common standards in the United States: Pedagogical implications for English learners. *TESOL Quarterly, 48*(3), 533–559.

Busse, V. (2011). Why do first-year students of German lose motivation during their first year at university? *Studies in Higher Education, 38*(7), 951–971.

Byrnes, H. (2009). Emergent L2 German writing ability in a curricular context: A longitudinal study of grammatical metaphor. *Linguistics and Education, 20*(1), 50–66.

Byrnes, H., Maxim, H. H., & Norris, J. M. (2010). Realizing advanced foreign language writing development in collegiate education: Curricular design, pedagogy, assessment. *The Modern Language Journal, 94*(Suppls–1).

Caplan, N. A. (2010). Beyond the five paragraph essay: A content-first approach. In S. Krashen (Ed.), *Effective second language writing*. Alexandria, VA: TESOL.

Carrell, P. L. (1984). The effects of rhetorical organization on ESL readers. *TESOL Quarterly, 18*(3), 441–469.

Carrell, P. L. (1987). Content and formal schemata in ESL reading. *TESOL Quarterly, 21*(3), 461–481.

Carter, R., & McCarthy, M. (in press). Spoken grammar: Where are we and where are we going? *Applied Linguistics* (Advance access).

Chang, A. C. S. (2009). Gains to L2 listeners from reading while listening vs. listening only in comprehending short stories. *System*, *37*(4), 652–663.

Chang, A. C. S., & Millett, S. (2015). Improving reading rates and comprehension through audio-assisted extensive reading for beginner learners. *System*, *52*, 91–102.

Chang, A. C. S., & Read, J. (2006). The effects of listening support on the listening performance of EFL learners. *TESOL Quarterly*, *40*(2), 375–397.

Cho, K. S., & Krashen, S. D. (1994). Acquisition of vocabulary from the Sweet Valley Kids series: Adult ESL acquisition. *Journal of Reading*, *37*, 662–667.

Chu, H. C. J., Swaffar, J., & Charney, D. H. (2002). Cultural representations of rhetorical conventions: The effects on reading recall. *TESOL Quarterly*, *36*(4), 511–541.

Claridge, G. (2005). Simplification in graded readers: Measuring the authenticity of graded texts. *Reading in a Foreign Language*, *17*(2), 144–158.

Cook, G. (2001). 'The philosopher pulled the lower jaw of the hen'. Ludicrous invented sentences in language teaching. *Applied Linguistics*, *22*(3), 366–387.

Coxhead, A. (2000). A new academic word list. *TESOL Quarterly*, *34*(2), 213–238.

Crossley, S. A., Allen, D., & McNamara, D. S. (2012). Text simplification and comprehensible input: A case for an intuitive approach. *Language Teaching Research*, *16*(1), 89–108.

Crossley, S. A., Louwerse, M. M., McCarthy, P. M., & McNamara, D. S. (2007). A linguistic analysis of simplified and authentic texts. *The Modern Language Journal*, *91*(1), 15–30.

Crossley, S. A., & McNamara, D. S. (2008). Assessing L2 reading texts at the intermediate level: An approximate replication of Crossley, Louwerse, McCarthy, & McNamara (2007). *Language Teaching*, *41*(3), 409–429.

Crossley, S. A., Yang, H. S., & McNamara, D. S. (2014). What's so simple about simplified texts? A computational and psycholinguistic investigation of text comprehension and text processing. *Reading in a Foreign Language, 26*(1), 92–113.

Cullen, R., & Kuo, I. (2007). Spoken grammar and ELT course materials: a missing link?. *TESOL Quarterly, 41*(2), 361–386.

Darhower, M. (2014). Literary discussions and advanced-superior speaking functions in the undergraduate language program. *Hispania, 97*(3), 396–412.

Davidheiser, J. C. (2007). Fairy tales and foreign languages: Ever the twain shall meet. *Foreign Language Annals, 40*(2), 215–225.

Davies, M. (2002). *Corpus del Español*. Retrieved from http://www.corpusdelespanol.org

Day, R. R., & Bamford, J. (1998). *Extensive reading in the second language classroom*. New York: Cambridge University Press.

DeKeyser, R. M. (2005). What makes learning second-language grammar difficult? A review of issues. *Language Learning, 55*(S1), 1–25.

Eisenchlas, S. A. (2011). On-line interactions as a resource to raise pragmatic awareness. *Journal of Pragmatics, 43*(1), 51–61.

Ellis, N. C., & Wulff, S. (2015). Second language acquisition. In E. Dabrowska, & D. Divjak (Eds.), *Handbook of cognitive linguistics* (pp. 409–431). Boston: DeGruyter Mouton.

Ellis, R. (2000). Task-based research and language pedagogy. *Language Teaching Research, 4*, 193–200.

Ellis, R. (2003). *Task-based language learning and teaching*. Oxford, U.K.: Oxford University Press.

Ellis, R. (2006). Current issues in the teaching of grammar: An SLA perspective. *TESOL Quarterly, 40*(1), 83–107.

Erten, I. H., & Razi, S. (2009). The effects of cultural familiarity on reading comprehension. *Reading in a Foreign Language, 21*(1), 60–77.

Feak, C. B., & Swales, J. M. (2009). *Telling a research story: Writing a literature review*. Ann Arbor: University of Michigan Press.

Fernández, C. (2011). Approaches to grammar instruction in teaching materials: A study in current L2 beginning-level Spanish textbooks. *Hispania, 94*(1), 155–170.

Fernández-Guerra, A. B., & Martínez-Flor, A. (2003). Requests in films and in EFL textbooks: A comparison. *Elia: Estudios de lingüística inglesa aplicada, 4*, 17–34.

Field, J. (2003). Promoting perception: Lexical segmentation in L2 listening. *ELT Journal, 57*(4), 325–334.

Folse, K. S. (2004). *Vocabulary myths: Applying second language research to classroom teaching.* Ann Arbor: University of Michigan Press.

Frantzen, D. (2013). Using literary texts to reveal problematic rules of usage. *Foreign Language Annals, 46*(4), 628–645.

Gabrielatos, C. (2005). Corpora and language teaching: Just a fling, or wedding bells?. *TESL-EJ, 8*(4), 1–37.

Gardner, D. (2008). Vocabulary recycling in children's authentic reading materials: A corpus-based investigation of narrow reading. *Reading in a Foreign Language, 20*(1), 92–122.

Gardner, D., & Hansen, E. C. (2007). Effects of lexical simplification during unaided reading of English informational texts. *TESL Reporter, 40*(2), 27–59.

Gass, S. M. 1997. Input, interaction and the second language learner. Mahwah, NJ: Lawrence Erlbaum.

Gilmore, A. (2007). Authentic materials and authenticity in foreign language learning. *Language Teaching, 40*(2), 97–118.

Gilmore, A. (2011). "I prefer not text": Developing Japanese learners' communicative competence with authentic materials. *Language Learning, 61*(3), 786–819.

Glisan, E. W. (2012). National standards: Research into practice. *Language Teaching, 45*(4), 515–526.

Goodall, G. (2010). Input from Spanish textbooks: Two case studies of poverty/richness of the stimulus. In C. Borgonovo, M. Español-Echevarría, & P. Prévost (Eds.), *Selected proceedings of the 12th Hispanic linguistics symposium* (pp. 260–269). Somerville, MA: Cascadilla Proceedings Project.

Grant, L., & Starks, D. (2001). Screening appropriate teaching materials: Closings from textbooks and television soap operas. *IRAL-International Review of Applied Linguistics in Language Teaching, 39*(1), 39–50.

Helmer, K. A. (2014). "It's not real, it's just a story to learn Spanish": Understanding heritage language learner resistance in a Southwest charter high school. *Heritage Language Journal, 11*(3), 186–206.

Hershberger, R., Navey-Davis, S., & Borrás, G. A. (2011). *Plazas, 4th Edition*. Boston, MA: Heinle.

Hertel, T. J., & Harrington, S. (2015). Promoting cultural and linguistic competence with documentary film in Spanish. *Hispania, 98*(3), 549–569.

Howard, J., & Matsuo, N. (2014). Developing professional proficiency: A Monterey model. *Dialog on Language Instruction, 24*(1), 53–68.

Hyland, K., & Tse, P. (2007). Is there an "academic vocabulary"? *TESOL Quarterly, 41*(2), 235–253.

Jiang, X. (2012). Effects of discourse structure graphic organizers on EFL reading comprehension. *Reading in a Foreign Language, 24*(1), 84–105.

Johns, T. (1994) From printout to handout: grammar and vocabulary teaching in the context of data-driven learning. In T. Odlin (Ed.), *Perspectives on pedagogical grammar* (pp. 293–313). Cambridge, U.K.: Cambridge University Press.

Kaiser, M. (2011). New approaches to exploiting film in the foreign language classroom. *L2 Journal, 3*(2), 232–249.

Kang, E. (2015). Promoting L2 vocabulary learning through narrow reading. *RELC Journal, 46*(2), 165–179.

Katz, S. (2001). Teaching literary texts at the intermediate level: A structured input approach (ERIC document reproduction service No. ED481417).

Katz, S. (2002). Teaching literary texts at the intermediate level: A structured input approach. In V. Scott & H. Tucker (Eds.), *Second language acquisition and the literature classroom: Fostering dialogues* (pp. 151–168). Boston: Heinle.

Kennedy, C., & Miceli, T. (2010). Corpus-assisted creative writing: Introducing intermediate Italian learners to a corpus as a reference resource. *Language Learning & Technology, 14*(1), 28–44.

Keshavarz, M. H., Atai, M. R., & Ahmadi, H. (2007). Content schemata, linguistic simplification, and EFL readers' comprehension and recall. *Reading in a Foreign Language, 19*(1), 19–33.

Kingsbury, K. C. (2011). Rosaura a las diez en el aula: La gramática a través de la literatura. *Hispania, 94*(2), 329–347.

Kowal, M., & Swain, M. (1997). From semantic to syntactic processing: How can we promote it in the immersion classroom? In K. Johnson & M. Swain (Eds). *Immersion education: International perspectives* (pp. 284–309). Cambridge, U.K.: Cambridge University Press.

Krashen, S. (2004). The case for narrow reading. *Language Magazine 3*(5), 17–19.

Krashen, S. D., & Terrell, T. D. (1983). The natural approach. Oxford and San Francisco: Pergamon/Alemany Press.

Kweon, S. O., & Kim, H. R. (2008). Beyond raw frequency: Incidental vocabulary acquisition in extensive reading. *Reading in a Foreign Language, 20*(2), 191–215.

Larson, L. (2015). E-books and audiobooks: Extending the digital reading experience. *The Reading Teacher, 69*(2), 169–177.

Larsen-Freeman, D. (2003). *Teaching language: From grammar to grammaring.* Boston: Heinle & Heinle.

Larsen-Freeman, D. (2015). Research into practice: Grammar learning and teaching. *Language Teaching, 48*(2), 263–280.

Laufer, B., & Hulstijn, J. (2001). Incidental vocabulary acquisition in a second language: The construct of task-induced involvement. *Applied Linguistics, 22*(1), 1–26.

Leeser, M. J. (2007). Learner-based factors in L2 reading comprehension and processing grammatical form: Topic familiarity and working memory. *Language Learning, 57*(2), 229–270.

Leow, R. P. (1997). The effects of input enhancement and text length on adult L2 readers' comprehension and intake in second language acquisition. *Applied Language Learning, 8*(2), 151–82.

Li, J., & Schmitt, N. (2009). The acquisition of lexical phrases in academic writing: A longitudinal case study. *Journal of Second Language Writing, 18*(2), 85–102.

Lin, M. H., & Lee, J. Y. (2015). Data-driven learning: changing the teaching of grammar in EFL classes. *ELT Journal, 69*(3), 264–274.

Liu, D., & Jiang, P. (2009). Using a corpus-based lexicogrammatical approach to grammar instruction in EFL and ESL contexts. *The Modern Language Journal, 93*(1), 61–78.

Llanes, À., & Muñoz, C. (2013). Age effects in a study abroad context: Children and adults studying abroad and at home. *Language Learning, 63*(1), 63–90.

Long, M.H. (1996). The role of the linguistic environment in second language acquisition. In W. C. Ritchie & T. K. Bhatia (Eds.), *Handbook of research on language acquisition* (pp. 413–468). New York: Academic Press.

Long, M. H. (2007). *Problems in SLA*. Mahwah, NJ: Lawrence Erlbaum.

Long, M. H. (2015). *Second language acquisition and task-based language teaching*. Malden, MA: Wiley-Blackwell.

Lynch, T. (2007). Learning from the transcripts of an oral communication task. *English Language Teaching Journal, 61*, 311–320.

Mackey, A. (1999). Input, interaction and second language development: An empirical study of question formation in ESL. *Studies in Second Language Acquisition, 21*, 557–587.

Martínez-Flor, A. (2008). Analysing request modification devices in films: Implications for pragmatic learning in instructed foreign language contexts. In E. Alcón Soler & M. P. Safont Jordà (Eds.), *Intercultural language use and language learning* (pp. 245–279). Amsterdam: Springer.

Maxim, H. (2002). A study into the feasibility and effects of reading extended authentic discourse in the beginning German language classroom. *The Modern Language Journal, 86*, 20–35.

Maxim, H. (2006). Integrating textual thinking into the introductory college-level foreign language classroom. *The Modern Language Journal, 90*, 19–32.

McCarthy, M., & Carter, R. (1995). Spoken grammar: What is it and how can we teach it? *ELT Journal, 49*(3), 207–218.

McCarthy, M., & Carter, R. (2002). Ten criteria for a spoken grammar. In E. Hinkel & S. Fotos (Eds.), *New perspectives on grammar teaching in second language classrooms* (pp. 51–75). Mahwah, NJ: Lawrence Erlbaum.

Millar, N., Budgell, B., & Fuller, K. (2013). 'Use the active voice whenever possible': The impact of style guidelines in medical journals. *Applied Linguistics, 34*, 393–414.

Miquel, L. & Sans, N. (2003). *Una nota falsa.* Barcelona: Difusión, Centro de Investigación y Publicaciones de Idiomas, S.L.

Mishan, F. (2004). Authenticating corpora for language learning: A problem and its resolution. *ELT Journal, 58*(3), 219–227.

Modern Language Association (2007). Foreign languages and higher education: New structures for a changed world. *Profession,* 234–245.

Mojica-Díaz, C. C., & Sánchez-López, L. (2010). Constructivist grammatical learning: A proposal for advanced grammatical analysis for college foreign language students. *Foreign Language Annals, 43*(3), 470–487.

Morrow, K. (1977). Authentic texts and ESP. In S. Holden (Ed.), *English for specific purposes* (pp. 13–17). London: Modern English Publications.

Myskow, G., & Gordon, K. (2009). A focus on purpose: Using a genre approach in an EFL writing class. *ELT Journal, 64*(3), 283–292.

Nakanishi, T. (2015). A meta-analysis of extensive reading research. *TESOL Quarterly, 49*(1), 6–37.

Nation, I. S. (2006). How large a vocabulary is needed for reading and listening? *Canadian Modern Language Review, 63*, 59–82.

Nation, P. (2015). Principles guiding vocabulary learning through extensive reading. *Reading in a Foreign Language, 27*(1), 136–145.

Nation, I. S. P., & Deweerdt, J. P. (2001). A defence of simplification. *Prospect, 16*(3), 55–64.

Nguyen, T. T. M. (2013). Instructional effects on the acquisition of modifiers in constructive criticism by EFL learners. *Language Awareness, 22*, 76–94.

Norris, J. M. (2009). Task-based teaching and testing. In M. Long & C. Doughty (Eds.), *The handbook of language teaching* (pp. 578–594). Malden, MA: Wiley-Blackwell.

Norris, J. M., & Ortega, L. (2000). Effectiveness of L2 instruction: A research synthesis and quantitative meta analysis. *Language Learning, 50*(3), 417–528.

O'Donnell, M. E. (2009). Finding middle ground in second language reading: Pedagogic modifications that increase comprehensibility and vocabulary acquisition while preserving authentic text features. *The Modern Language Journal, 93*(4), 512–533.

Oh, S. Y. (2001). Two types of input modification and EFL reading comprehension: Simplification versus elaboration. *TESOL Quarterly, 35*(1), 69–96.

O'Keefe, A., McCarthy, M., & Carter, R. (2007). *From corpus to classroom: Language use and language teaching.* New York: Cambridge University Press.

Oller, J. W. (1995). Adding abstract to formal and content schema. Results of recent work in Peircean semiotics. *Applied Linguistics, 16,* 273–306.

O'Sullivan, Í., & Chambers, A. (2006). Learners' writing skills in French: Corpus consultation and learner evaluation. *Journal of Second Language Writing, 15*(1), 49–68.

Paesani, K. (2005). Literary texts and grammar instruction: Revisiting the inductive presentation. *Foreign Language Annals, 38*(1), 15–23.

Parker, K., & Chaudron, C. (1987). The effects of linguistic simplification and elaborative modifications on L2 comprehension. *University of Hawai'i Working Papers in ESL, 6,* 107–133.

Pellicer-Sánchez, A., & Schmitt, N. (2010). Incidental vocabulary acquisition from an authentic novel: Do "things fall apart"? *Reading in a Foreign Language, 22*(1), 31–55.

Pennac, D. (2006). *The rights of the reader.* London: Walker Books.

Pica, T. (1994). Research on negotiation: What does it reveal about second language learning conditions, processes, and outcomes? *Language Learning, 44,* 493–527.

Pica, T. (2002). Subject-matter content: How does it assist the interactional and linguistic needs of classroom language learners? *The Modern Language Journal, 86*(1), 1–19.

Pica, T., Kanagy, R., & Falodun, J. (1993). Choosing and using communication tasks for second language instruction and research. In G. Crookes & S. M. Gass (Eds.), *Tasks and language learning: Integrating theory and practice* (pp. 9–34). Clevedon, U.K.: Multilingual Matters.

Polio, C., & Zyzik, E. (2009). Don Quixote meets *ser* and *estar*: Multiple perspectives on language learning in Spanish literature classes. *The Modern Language Journal, 93*(4), 550–569.

Prince, P. (2013). Listening, remembering, writing: Exploring the dictogloss task. *Language Teaching Research, 17*, 486–500.

Pulido, D. (2007). The effects of topic familiarity and passage sight vocabulary on L2 lexical inferencing and retention through reading. *Applied Linguistics, 28*(1), 66–86.

Quinn, C. (2015). Training L2 writers to reference corpora as a self-correction tool. *ELT Journal, 69*(2), 165–177.

Redmann, J. (2005). An interactive reading journal for all levels of the foreign language curriculum. *Foreign Language Annals, 38*(4), 484–492.

Redmann, J. (2008). Reading Kästner's Emil und die Detektive in the context of a literacy oriented curriculum. *Die Unterrichtspraxis/ Teaching German, 41*(1), 72–81.

Reinhardt, J. (2010). The potential of corpus-informed pedagogy. *Studies in Hispanic and Lusophone Linguistics, 3*(1), 239–251.

Richards, J. C., & Reppen, R. (2014). Towards a pedagogy of grammar instruction. *RELC Journal, 45*(1), 5–25.

Roberts, C., & Cooke, M. (2009). Authenticity in the adult ESOL classroom and beyond. *TESOL Quarterly*, 620–642.

Rodgers, D. M. (2015). Incidental language learning in foreign language content courses. *The Modern Language Journal, 99*(1), 113–136.

Rodgers, M. P. (2013). English language learning through viewing television: An investigation of comprehension, incidental vocabulary acquisition, lexical coverage, attitudes, and captions (Unpublished dissertation). University of Wellington.

Rodgers, M. P., & Webb, S. (2011). Narrow viewing: The vocabulary in related television programs. *TESOL Quarterly, 45*(4), 689–717.

Römer, U. (2011). Corpus research applications in second language teaching. *Annual Review of Applied Linguistics, 31,* 205–225.

Rose, K. R. (2001). Compliments and compliment responses in film: Implications for pragmatics research and language teaching. *IRAL, 39*(4), 309–326.

Ross, S., Long, M. H., & Yano, Y. (1991). Simplification or elaboration? The effects of two types of text modifications on foreign language reading comprehension. *University of Hawai'i Working Papers in ESL, 10,* 1–32.

Ryshina-Pankova, M. (2011). Developmental changes in the use of interactional resources: Persuading the reader in FL book reviews. *Journal of Second Language Writing, 20*(4), 243–256.

Sato, C. (1990). *The syntax of conversation in interlanguage development.* Tübingen, Germany: Gunter Narr Verlag.

Schleppegrell, M. J., Achugar, M., & Oteíza, T. (2004). The grammar of history: Enhancing content based instruction through a functional focus on language. *TESOL Quarterly, 38*(1), 67–93.

Schmitt, N., Jiang, X., & Grabe, W. (2011). The percentage of words known in a text and reading comprehension. *The Modern Language Journal, 95*(1), 26–43.

Schmitt, N. (2008). Review article: Instructed second language vocabulary learning. *Language Teaching Research, 12*(3), 329–363.

Schmitt, N., & Carter, R. (2000). The lexical advantages of narrow reading for second language learners. *TESOL Journal 9*(1), 4–9.

Shanahan, T., Fisher, D., & Frey, N. (2012). The challenge of challenging text. *Educational Leadership, 69*(2), 58–62.

Simpson-Vlach, R., & Ellis, N. (2010). An academic formulas list: New methods in phraseology research. *Applied Linguistics, 31*(4), 487–512.

Skehan, P. (1998). *A cognitive approach to language learning.* Oxford, U.K.: Oxford University Press.

Smart, J. (2014). The role of guided induction in paper-based data-driven learning. *ReCALL, 26*(2), 184–201.

Spada, N. (1997). Form-focused instruction and second language acquisition: A review of classroom and laboratory research. *Language Teaching, 30*(2), 73–87.

Steffensen, M. S., Joag-Dev, C., & Anderson, R. C. (1979). A cross-cultural perspective on reading comprehension. *Reading Research Quarterly, 15*(1), 10–29.

Sundquist, J. (2010). The long and short of it: The use of short films in the German classroom. *Die Unterrichtspraxis/Teaching German, 43*(2), 123–132.

Swaffar, J. K. (1985). Reading authentic texts in a foreign language: A cognitive model. *The Modern Language Journal, 69*(1), 15–34.

Swaffar, J. K., & Arens, K. (2005). *Remapping the foreign language curriculum: An approach through multiple literacies.* New York: Modern Language Association of America.

Swain, M. (2005) The output hypothesis: theory and research. In E. Hinkel (Ed.). *Handbook of research in second language teaching and learning* (p. 471–484). Mahwah, NJ: Lawrence Erlbaum.

Swain, M. (1985). Communicative competence: Some roles of comprehensible input and comprehensible output in its development. In S. Gass & C. Madden (Eds.), *Input in second language acquisition* (pp. 235–253). Rowley, MA: Newbury House.

Swales, J. (1990). *Genre analysis: English in academic and research settings.* New York: Cambridge University Press.

Swales, J. M. (2005). Attended and unattended "this" in academic writing: A long and unfinished story. *ESP Malaysia, 11*(1), 1–15.

Swales, J. M., & Feak, C. B. (2011). *Navigating academia: Writing supporting genres.* Ann Arbor: University of Michigan Press.

Takimoto, M. (2008). The effects of deductive and inductive instruction on the development of language learners' pragmatic competence. *The Modern Language Journal, 92*, 369–386.

Timmis, I. (2005). Towards a framework for teaching spoken grammar. *ELT Journal, 59*(2), 117–125.

Tognozzi, E. (2010). Teaching and evaluating language and culture through film. *Italica, 87*(1), 69–91.

Tweissi, A. I. (1998). The effects of the amount and type of simplification on foreign language reading comprehension. *Reading in a Foreign Language, 11*(2), 191–204.

Tyler, A. (2010). Usage-based approaches to language and their applications to second language learning. *Annual Review of Applied Linguistics, 30,* 270–291.

Uden, J., Schmitt, D., & Schmitt, N. (2014). Jumping from the highest graded readers to ungraded novels: Four case studies. *Reading in a Foreign Language, 26*(1), 1–28.

Van den Branden, K. (2000). Does negotiation of meaning promote reading comprehension? A study of multilingual primary school classes. *Reading Research Quarterly, 35*(3), 426–443.

Van den Branden, K. (2006). Introduction: Task-based language teaching in a nutshell. In K. Van den Branden (Ed.), *Task-based language education* (pp. 1–16). Cambridge, U.K.: Cambridge University Press.

Vanderplank, R. (2010). *Déjà vu?* A decade of research on language laboratories, television and video in language learning. *Language Teaching, 43,* 1–37.

Verspoor, M., & Smiskova, H. (2012). Foreign language writing development from a dynamic usage based perspective. In R. Manchón (Ed). *L2 writing development: Multiple perspectives* (pp. 17–46) Boston: DeGruyter Mouton.

Vogel, S., Herron, C., Cole, S. P., & York, H. (2011). Effectiveness of a guided inductive versus a deductive approach on the learning of grammar in the intermediate-level college French classroom. *Foreign Language Annals, 44*(2), 353–380.

Wagner, E. (2014). Using unscripted spoken texts in the teaching of second language listening. *TESOL Journal, 5*(2), 288–311.

Wang, C., & Wang, M. (2014). Effect of alignment on L2 written production. *Applied Linguistics, 36,* 503–526.

Washburn, G. N. (2001). Using situation comedies for pragmatic language teaching and learning. *TESOL Journal, 10*(4), 21–26.

Webb, S. (2014). Repetition in incidental vocabulary learning. In C. Chappelle (Ed.), *Encyclopedia of applied linguistics* (pp. 1–6). Oxford, U.K.: Wiley-Blackwell.

Webb, S. (2015). Extensive viewing: language learning through watching television. In D. Nunan & J.C. Richards (Eds.), *Language learning beyond the classroom* (pp. 159–168). New York: Routledge.

Webb, S., & Chang, A. C. S. (2015). Second language vocabulary learning through extensive reading with audio support: How do frequency and distribution of occurrence affect learning? *Language Teaching Research, 19*(6), 667–686.

Webb, S., Newton, J., & Chang, A. C. S. (2013). Incidental learning of collocation. *Language Learning, 63*, 91–120.

Weyers, J. R. (1999). The effect of authentic video on communicative competence. *The Modern Language Journal, 83*(3), 339–349.

Widdowson, H. G. (1998). Context, community, and authentic language. *TESOL Quarterly, 32*(4), 705–716.

Widdowson, H. G. (2004). *Text, context, pretext*. London: Blackwell.

Williams, J. (2012). The potential role(s) of writing in second language development. *Journal of Second Language Writing, 21*, 321–331.

Willis, J. (2004). Perspectives on task-based instruction: Understanding our practices, acknowledging different practitioners. In B. Leaver & J. Willis (Eds.), *Task-based instruction in foreign language education* (pp. 3–46). Washington, DC: Georgetown University Press.

Wong Fillmore, L. (2014). English language learners at the crossroads of educational reform. *TESOL Quarterly, 48*(3), 624–632.

Wong Fillmore, L., & Fillmore, C. (2012, January). What does text complexity mean for English language learners and language minority students? Paper presented at the Understanding Language Conference, Stanford, CA. Retrieved from http://ell.stanford.edu/papers/language

Yang, A. (2001). Reading and the non-academic learner: A mystery solved. *System, 29*(4), 451–466.

Yano, Y., Long, M. H., & Ross, S. (1994). The effects of simplified and elaborated texts on foreign language reading. *Language Learning, 44*(2), 189–219.

Yasuda, S. (2011). Genre-based tasks in foreign language writing: Developing writers' genre awareness, linguistic knowledge, and writing competence. *Journal of Second Language Writing, 20*(2), 111–133.

Young, D. J. (1999). Linguistic simplification of SL reading material: Effective instructional practice? *The Modern Language Journal, 83*(3), 350–366.

Zyzik, E., & Polio, C. (2008). Incidental focus on form in university Spanish literature courses. *The Modern Language Journal, 92*(1), 53–70.

Index

Abrams, Z. I., 61, 78–79, 117
Academic Word List, 69
activating background knowledge.
   See background knowledge
adult immigrants studying ESL,
   134–135
advanced-level learners, 8, 21, 52, 64,
   131–132; data-driven learning
   and, 40; grammar instruction,
   34–35, 75; productive skills, 82,
   83, 85, 88–89, 125; vocabulary
   instruction, 69, 74
Allen, E. D., 51, 95
Alpetkin, C., 19, 65
Arens, K., 24–25
audio-assisted reading, 14, 61–62,
   114, 119–120, 124
audiolingual method, 5
authentic materials: choosing, 9–10,
   12, 23–24; defined, 1–2; historical
   context for use, 5–6; practical
   problems for use, 9–10; reasons
   for use, 6–9; types of, 2–4

background knowledge, activation of
   and materials, 63–75; comprehension and, 101, 102, 103–104,
   106, 107; difficult language,
   68–71; formal schema, 64, 67–68;
   grammar and, 64, 68–71; material
   choice (length), 59–60; practical
   solutions, 72–75, 107–108; pre-
   reading and pre-listening tasks,

18, 41–42, 63–64, 66; thematic
   continuity, 55, 57; topic and
   cultural familiarity, 64, 65–67;
   vocabulary and, 64, 68–71
Barbieri, F., 42, 118–119
Bartlett, L., 133
beginning-level learners, 13–26, 125;
   activity choice, 14–15, 20–21,
   24–25; collaborative study of,
   17–18, 20; content-based
   instruction for, 8; familiarity of
   subject/genre, 14, 18–19, 23–24;
   infographics, 25; materials choice
   and, 20, 23–24; motivation and,
   15; narrow reading, 22; repetition
   and, 14–15, 19, 22; true
   beginners, 13, 17–18
Benavides, C., 39–40
Bernhardt, E. B., 15–16, 51, 107–108
Boulton, A., 40–41, 44
Byrnes, H., 85–86, 90–91

Caplan, N. A., 84
Carrell, P. L., 67
Carter, R., 22, 41–42, 43, 54, 81
Chang, A. C. S., 62, 67, 68–69, 113
character-based languages, 12, 136
Charney, D. H., 67–68
Chu, H. C. J., 67–68
cloze activities, 6, 88, 114, 123
collaborative learning, 17–18, 20
collocations, 33, 69, 113
Common Core State Standards, 49